D1590718

MEAN BUSINESS

MEAN BUSINESS

The Insider's Guide to
Winning Any Political Election

MATT TOWERY
& PIERRE HOWARD

LONGSTREET PRESS

Published by
LONGSTREET PRESS
2140 Newmarket Parkway
Suite 122
Marietta, GA 30067

Printed in the United States of America

1st printing 2000

Library of Congress Catalog Card Number: 99-068605

ISBN: 1-56352-608-5

Jacket design by Burtch Hunter
Book design by Megan Wilson

Visit Longstreet Press on the World Wide Web
www.longstreetpress.net

The best is yet to come.

TABLE OF CONTENTS

MEAN BUSINESS

WE KNOW. . . .
WE'VE BEEN THERE

There is no cure for it other than embalming fluid, or at least that's how the saying goes. "It" is the political bug—the game that creates the desire to run, to watch, and to win. The problem is, American politics is no longer a game. Political races, be they for president of the United States or for the local school board, have generated a multi-million-dollar industry. With that much money on the table, what used to be a semidignified pursuit of power has turned into the biggest and meanest of businesses. Add in the factor of near-instant communication and fund-raising capabilities brought about by the Internet, and it's a mean business increasingly conducted at lightning speed.

And unlike most businesses, this one has relatively few experts who really understand how to apply the same principles that enabled, say, a General Electric to grow from simple purveyors of the light bulb to a multiservice corporation of massive proportions—or enabled a computer software company created in a Seattle garage to grow into the giant known as Microsoft.

And politics, when you think about it, is the most dangerous business of them all. No other industry is as open to public scrutiny or criticism. Even the winners are often ultimate losers, both in their finite terms in office and their negative perceptions among the public. Fail to negotiate the course with precision, and even the most entrenched career official can find the party over.

We know this firsthand because we've been there ourselves. We aren't jaded academics in some ivory tower; we've been on the front-line, fighting in the trenches. And we can assure you, it's not a fight for the faint of heart.

We have participated in the political process not only as advisors and insiders, but as candidates who once squared off against each other for the office of lieutenant governor. Now we're partners in an effort to bring the equalizing power of the Internet to play in the arena of political affairs, working with individuals and businesses to transform how the business of government gets done. It's been quite an experience, combining old-fashioned yard-sign politics with Web sites and pop-up boxes, television commercials with banner ads. It has enabled us to realize that we are standing on the leading edge of an explosive communications revolution that is already forever changing the way individuals and businesses interact with the systems of politics and government.

In this book, we intend to show you not only how to run an effective campaign based upon principles from the business world, and how to apply some campaign principles to the business side of government, but also to address some of the changes the age of "dot.coms" is bringing to these processes. We'll also let you in on all the secrets of rough-and-tumble campaigning that we've experienced firsthand. Read this book and you'll learn all about "street money," "advocacy polling," "slick sheets," "opposition research," "voter suppression"—and every other trick you may or may not have heard of. Believe us, they all exist. We've seen it all, from fistfights, to lawsuits, to opposing consultants sharing last-minute polling data—not to help their candidates, but to cover their own rear ends. We each met up with virtually every vicious commercial and crackpot activist imaginable. We were shaken down for money by all sorts—ranging from self-proclaimed pollsters to "concerned" members of the clergy asking for "love offerings"—and faced everything from standing ovations to death threats.

If only we had known some of the secrets of this mean business ahead of time, we could have gone into politics with our eyes a bit more wide open. As it was, our respective campaigns for Georgia lieutenant governor were important learning experiences for us both.

☆ ☆ ☆ ☆ ☆

PIERRE: In 1990, Matt Towery was a young lawyer who had served ten years earlier as an up-and-coming speechwriter in the biggest Republican upset in modern Southern politics—the defeat of Herman Talmadge by businessman Mack Mattingly. Matt went on to become an early protégé and advisor to the rising bad boy of his party, Newt Gingrich. Gingrich had chosen Matt because of Matt's prior national success as a champion debater.

Along the way Matt worked with old-time GOP consultants—names like Wilma Goldstein, Melinda and Bob Weed, and Joe Gaylord. They asked him to help teach breakout courses at the NRCC's Congressional Candidate school. The young Matt had in his very first class a then-mustachioed and green candidate with a standout name—Connie Mack. Mack would go on to become both a congressman and U.S. senator from Florida.

And Matt? Well, he would go on to face the impossible—and what he perhaps considered the foolish—task of winning his party's nomination to be lieutenant governor of Georgia.

MATT: By 1990, Georgia was rapidly becoming one of America's ten most populated states. We had no idea what we were getting into in our respective bids for lieutenant governor. In earlier years, the office had been a throwaway race. But times were changing and there was an awful lot of money involved.

My chief opponent was a sixteen-year veteran of the Georgia State Senate, this man with the most un–Georgia-like name of Pierre Howard. I knew that Pierre was telegenic and well connected through his years in politics. The Howard family had, for generations, been an integral part of Georgia Democratic politics. Pierre had earned a reputation for defending the elderly, protecting the environment, and working to make Georgia government more open.

And because the state was still heavily Democratic, Pierre faced a parade of opponents, including a popular state senator with a good-ole-boy look, but a very progressive name: Joe Kennedy.

Kennedy, an affable and gentle man who has since died, had the power of the state's political establishment behind him from his years as president pro tem of the state senate. And that name Kennedy was likely to confuse many core Democratic voters who might assume he was one of "the" Kennedys.

Pierre fought the misconception with a series of well-produced ads that pictured him standing at the edge of a river, his youthful face speaking of the need to preserve Georgia's environment, a cause about which he was a bit obsessed. And when Pierre and Joe Kennedy faced off in a runoff for the Democratic nomination, Pierre's media advisors went for the obvious: the "comparison ad." They took every non-progressive, out-of-step vote Joe ever made and reminded voters "He's no Kennedy."

PIERRE: And as for the rural voters, for whom my "fancy" French name might be an electoral turnoff, our answer came right out of Republican Ronald Reagan's playbook. My standard line (repeated ad nauseum) was "Pierre is French for 'Bubba.'" The line always received overwhelming laughter—except from Matt, who had heard it hundreds of times!

In the meantime, Matt was barely old enough to constitutionally serve as lieutenant governor, and was seeking the nomination of a party that had not won the governorship (much less the "lite governorship," as they called it) since Reconstruction. I think I was actually the least of his concerns; Matt was consumed with the bane of every Republican's existence: intraparty politics.

MATT: It was rough. While I had the tacit endorsement of Georgia's then-lone GOP congressman, Newt Gingrich, I was met with little enthusiasm by the Republican front-runner for governor, then-House Majority Leader (and now my very close friend and Congressman) Johnny Isakson. Isakson had been convinced by his campaign manager that a Towery candidacy, coming from the same home county as Isakson, would be detrimental. Add to that the fact that Pierre was Isakson's fraternity brother, and it was clear that I had stumbled into hostile territory!

As a newcomer with no political experience, I also made all the typical first-timer mistakes, like buying lots of radio time in the dead of winter, long before anyone even knew we had a race going on.

PIERRE: I made my share, too. I was convinced that I needed to attend every speaking engagement and every public forum, no matter how distant or small. By the end of the campaign I was utterly exhausted. I remember driving from Atlanta to Folkston, Georgia, on the Florida state line, for a barbeque and returning the same night—a total distance of some five hundred miles—getting home at 3 A.M. only to face a 7:30 breakfast the next morning.

MATT: My biggest mistake was not spending my money on positive name identification ads in order to set myself up for a stronger future. Instead, I wasted dollars on a scattershot attack on a few of Pierre's earlier votes as a senator. It fell on deaf ears. By October, we had both secured our respective party nominations. But it was clear that the Democrats would far outdistance the GOP.

PIERRE: Matt whipped my behind in our one statewide debate, but no one was watching.

MATT: A week later Pierre whipped mine in what really mattered, the general election.
PIERRE: Matt called to congratulate me within the first hour after the polls closed. But both of us remained friendly. We had run clean campaigns—no personal attacks.

MATT: We both went on to serve in Georgia's general assembly— working together as friends.

PIERRE: I pushed legislation naming a state bridge after Matt, who had run Newt Gingrich's toughest race, and who had served as strategist against James Carville and Paul Begala in a 1994 Georgia governor's race that was decided by less than thirty-five thousand votes.

MATT: I was there on the podium the night Pierre accepted the thunderous applause of a Senate chamber over which he had successfully presided for eight years. He had been leading all names as a virtual shoo-in for Georgia's next governor the previous year, when he had come to the same conclusion I had reached a year before: that there was a cure for the political bug other than embalming fluid—it's called "walking away."

And so here we are, both working and writing together as a team. And unlike so many who pontificate and prognosticate in the world of politics, we are different. No one will deny that Matt Towery was in the room of no more than ten people when it was put to then-President George Bush that he had to publicly admit that his decision to raise taxes in 1991 was a mistake. Three days later he did just that. And many remember how Pierre Howard worked for Jimmy Carter when the then-unknown governor was just launching his bid to be president. Those who know, know that Matt sat with Newt Gingrich, his two lawyers, and his friend Mack Mattingly in Gingrich's private office moments before he went to the House floor to accept a tepid reelection as Speaker in 1996. The vote had followed a deeply divisive ethics inquiry of Gingrich.

So trust us when we say that a secret world surrounds the electoral process. The very best operatives know their counterparts—some, such as Republican Mary Matalin and Democrat James Carville, even go so far as to share a marriage. But this doesn't mean that, when it comes to doing battle, even spouses on opposing teams aren't capable of taking the field and using every trick of the trade to do their loved one's candidate harm.

If you choose to strap on the pads and play this hardest of "hardball" (as Chris Matthews of CNBC has so aptly labeled it), be prepared—you will get hit. The political process of the new millennium is so tough that even the most devout religious leaders and the most pure of heart civic activists suddenly find themselves tempted to use obscenities. And if you believe this is an overly cynical view of the process, then close this book right now and, for goodness sake, don't run for public office.

POLITICS . . . "THE REAL WORLD"

There are some hard, basic realities that any candidate for public office in the United States must confront. There are some others that their spouses, friends, supporters, and staff must also be aware of—before a run for office is begun. First, the candidates.

Candidate Reality #1

It's all about money, but money alone will not guarantee victory.

The days when Mr. Smith could get to Washington (or even get a seat on the local school board) propelled simply by a desire to do good, or with the backing of some strong political machine, are over. Cash is the new king. And whether it's the ability to buy more signs and drop more mail in a local race, or purchase twice the number of gross rating points (a television term we'll explain a little later) in a U.S. senate or presidential primary, there is a high correlation between placing first on the fund-raising front and placing first in the ultimate electoral vote.

Those who are shy about asking—even begging—for money must learn to overcome their reluctance or face destruction. The good news is that most candidates, no matter how proud or reticent, can and do overcome this barrier. Some, such as former U.S. Senator Alfonse D'Amato of New York, not only become good at raising money, they come to embrace it with the same enthusiasm that most athletes have for their chosen sport! (D'Amato was still half-jokingly soliciting funds to cover the debt from his 1998 defeat in a *George* magazine column a year later.) This book is designed to help those who have yet to reach such levels of confidence.

There are those rare candidates who have enough money to fund their campaigns almost or entirely on their own. The good news for them is that they can skip the section on fund-raising. The bad news is that often they are not victorious and thus cannot rely on the general tenet that the candidate with the most money wins; there are exceptions to every rule.

The most common reason is that candidates who are self-funded usually come from two camps: spoiled rich kids who never really had to work or deal with the real world, and self-made men or women who believe they can translate their success in other disciplines into success in the world of politics. What a laugh! The national political scene makes even the highest levels of corporate life look like powder-puff football.

That's not to say that a businesslike approach to politics is a bad thing. Indeed, we strongly believe it is the missing secret ingredient to success for most campaigns. But—as is the case with most businesses—producing the product, marketing it, and reaping the desired rewards is far more complicated than it appears; to be successful, one must rely on a "corporate structure" that includes individuals with highly specialized technical skills. It's the corporate structure and discipline that most campaigns lack. And, as we will show you in this book, that structure is not so very hard to create. You just have to know the right steps.

There's been a lot of talk during the 2000 election cycle about the potential of using the Internet as a fund-raising tool, and how the "Internet factor" may change the fiscal landscape of elections. We will address this later in the book, as well, but let us say up front that no smart candidate should go into any race—be it for that local school board seat or for president—relying upon the Internet as his or her only mechanism for raising funds.

Candidate Reality #2
"Get ready to rumble!"

Some political observers like to suggest that campaigns and elections just recently became blood sports in which no subject or skeleton was left untouched. That's really not true. In fact, some of the nastiest presidential campaigns were waged in the 1800s. But certainly the early 1970s marked a change in the way in which the press approached its coverage of national political candidates. Ironically, that change began not with Richard Nixon and Watergate, but with Nixon's '72 opponent George McGovern's choice of vice-presidential nominee, Senator Thomas Eagleton. When word spread that Eagleton had received significant psychotherapy (including electroshock) in earlier years, the media ran with the story, and Eagleton was forced to resign from the ticket.

The real change in the "nastiness" of elections has taken place at the local and state levels. Even in the early 1980s, it would have been highly unlikely to see allegations concerning a candidate's private life surface to a level where it would impact the actual outcome of an election in any campaign, except those for the highest of offices.

In the twenty-first century, even the candidate for local school board or county commission can assume that allegations will be made, whether true or not, about some aspect of their personal or professional life. Bank on it. Those who are afraid to face a last minute "slick sheet" mailer full of mean and vicious allegations or misrepresentations about themselves should either follow the steps we outline in this book to anticipate and handle such attacks—or not bother running for office.

And if you think you are "too good" a person to go on the attack yourself, well, let's just say that we'll see how good you are by the end of your first campaign. You will be amazed at how quickly you will declare negative campaigning "self-defense," once you see your opponents lobbing nuclear bombs your way. The bottom line is that all campaigns have a strong dose of negative in them, whether they call it such or choose to cloak it in less offensive terms, such as "clarifying my opponent's position."

Candidate Reality #3
"If you want a friend in politics, get a dog!"

That famous quote, uttered (partly) in jest about life in Washington, D.C., applies to every level of politics in the new century. In reality, it is possible for political candidates to have friends, indeed many friends. But it's very difficult to have many close friends because of the tremendous constraints that running for and serving in office place on one's time.

If you expect to be loved and adored for all of your wonderful ideas and talents, forget it. You will attract many admirers and supporters along the way, and you will develop a small cadre of insiders who are both friends and voluntary advisors—but the life of a political candidate is a lonely and often defensive one.

Most of that defensiveness will be caused by your interaction with the media. We know what you're thinking. "I'm different, I'll make the media my friend." And while it is both possible and even likely that you will create good relations with some reporters, columnists, or publishers, there is no doubt that you will, from time to time, endure the hot grill and bitter sting that comes from an aggressive reporter or tough columnist or editorial board. And, as much as we both hated being on the receiving end of the media's barbs, we just as gleefully enjoyed commenting and opining at the expense of another candidate or elected official when the opportunity arose. We will do our best to explain what to do and say to protect yourself from the hardened professionals who cover politics, because they can be the unexpected enemy.

The Final Candidate Reality

If you never lose a race, you will be the exception . . . and we and everyone else in the political world will hate you!

. . . Out of unabashed jealousy, of course. That's because we know very few individuals who have found true success in the world of politics without encountering some huge bumps along the way. America has not had a president who did not experience some form of the "agony of defeat" since Dwight Eisenhower. Even John Kennedy suffered set-backs, such as his short-lived effort to be his party's vice-presidential nominee in 1956.

All of that being said, we do believe that this book offers any potential candidate, no matter how experienced, a clear blueprint on how to organize a successful campaign. We can't promise you an election victory in your first run for office, but we can give you the right tools to enter that first race with conviction. And even the most seasoned politician will learn an eye-opening thing or two from the many political pros who have taken the time to share on these pages their experiences, advice, and ideas. This book is an unabashedly politically incorrect, yet highly effective, tool for understanding the political process and its techniques, from the basic to the most secret and sophisticated. Our aim is to plant some good seeds in the head of anyone who is considering a race for public office so they can make an informed decision.

Since no candidate exists in a vacuum, there are of course other issues to be addressed concerning the people who surround every candidate: loved ones, friends, staff. We think it's important to mention their potential concerns up front as well, because, just like a business, an effective election campaign is a team effort all the way.

Advice for Spouses

Get on board now, or stage a mutiny . . . because once this ship sets sail,
you may never see dry land again.

Candidates rarely understand the true sacrifices that spouses or "significant others" make to accommodate their political careers. Some wives and husbands, boyfriends and girlfriends are as excited about the political process as their loved ones. But a much more significant segment of this "second banana" group must learn to acquire a taste for the political life—or at least learn to endure it with a smile.

The biggest problems that arise for families or couples during political campaigns center around two basic things: time and money. Personal time during a campaign is in short supply. The telephone never stops ringing, and whether it's a smaller race (in which the candidate spends half of his or her time putting up signs or trying to keep signs from being destroyed) or a bigger one that requires endless fundraisers and hairy rides in questionable small planes (oh, those planes!), there is never the luxury of balancing family and career in a way that we all would like. In our experience, the months of a campaign will, after the fact, take on the time-warpish characteristics of an extended bout with the flu.

However, there are ways to make the whole endeavor not only survivable but enjoyable. We are aware of how important the support of a spouse or other loved one is in being successful in this particular kind of business venture, so we will present these points as plainly as we can. Sometimes, just having some advance knowledge of exactly how difficult a situation might be is enough to help steel the heart of a reluctant spouse. But if you are the type of person who already knows that you simply cannot endure the life of a "politician's husband" (or wife or boyfriend/girlfriend), then now is the time to have a very special and intense discussion with the potential candidate. Most significant others ultimately decide they are up to the task. Many who enter the arena with doubts find that they actually enjoy being a part of the campaign. But a few simply cannot take it. Find out now where you stand; otherwise, the results could be catastrophic.

Advice for Campaign Volunteers
Get ready for a dose of reality.

Some of the kindest, nicest, most decent people in the world have been innocently sucked into the world of professional politics by starting out as a "simple" volunteer. Volunteers usually join political campaigns because they are friends of the candidate, have been politically active in the past, or are attracted by the candidate's position on the issues (imagine that!).

Volunteers need to understand that a campaign offers an incredible opportunity to learn about the "real world of politics," as well as create many valuable business, social, and civic relationships. The upside of being heavily involved in a political campaign can be significant.

That being said, volunteers should also understand that candidates change as the pressures of an election mount, and this change is only accelerated in the event that they are victorious. Time constraints and the inevitable ego-inflation that come with greater media attention are only magnified if the candidate succeeds. This applies to candidates seeking reelection as well.

If you are a volunteer in a campaign, you will observe and learn things that are entertaining, amazing, and invaluable. But you will also often feel unappreciated and sometimes even forgotten. Shake it off. If you actually believe that politicians can be your best friend, you will be disappointed; they simply have too many people to deal with and too little time.

This doesn't mean that you won't be important to them or that your involvement won't be valuable. And usually at least one volunteer in every campaign goes on to become a trusted assistant to a victorious candidate. Many others will land jobs on a victorious candidate's staff. But it is highly unlikely that you will have the same sort of friendship with a politician that you enjoy with other individuals.

Advice for Staffers
Stay above the fray and never agree to be the messenger—
they always get shot!

There is usually more political wrangling going on between staff members within a single campaign than there is between the political candidates themselves. The most successful campaigns are those that somehow manage to avoid such egotistical rivalries, or those where managers know how to take advantage of internal jealousies in order to keep everyone off balance—thus causing them to work harder for the candidate.

But most campaigns balkanize into various camps with secret meetings, late-night phone calls, and downright sabotage of one colleague or group of colleagues by another. The most successful staff worker manages to somehow avoid becoming a part of anyone's internal camp, or, alternately, seeks out and destroys his or her detractors at the outset. That's a vicious fact of life, but the rooting out of incompetent or downright bad campaign staff, consultants, pollsters, etc., can often be the only way to save a campaign in discord. Usually if there is severe infighting in a campaign, it arises over disagreements about basic strategy, issue development, or staffers' positions. And usually the group that wins the battle for control is the more politically skillful in general, and therefore more likely to deliver a well-run campaign.

No matter how intense the battling and no matter how strongly you may believe in your concepts or ideas, never be the messenger who delivers bad news to the candidate. Very few candidates appreciate or comprehend bad news during the heat of the campaign. Many times they will look back, months after their defeat, and recognize that they should have heeded the warnings of a bearer of bad news. But that does very little for the poor, unemployed former staffer.

Always find someone who has nothing to lose to deliver tough medicine that the candidate needs to hear. Then, jump in and build support for its acceptance. It's the only way to get panicked and confused candidates to listen and act for their own good.

MATT: I remember telling Newt Gingrich, just days before the vote, that I believed he might lose the GOP primary in 1992. He was so irritated with me that he scheduled a "two-year planning session" for the very hour the polls closed. Two hours later he was trailing a virtually unknown opponent. And although Newt emerged the winner in the narrowest of victories, I felt the enduring heat of having been the deliverer of an unwanted message.

Hopefully so far we've peaked your interest in the election process, and not simply scared you away. We want to give an honest portrait of American politics, but our intention is not to burst the bubble of every Speaker of the House wannabe. Our goal is to impart to you, the reader—whether you are a potential candidate for public office, the friend or staff of a potential candidate, or merely a politics buff—what we've learned during our exhilarating, exasperating, always-fascinating adventures in the political arena. While there is no substitute for experience, we can certainly say that we would have greatly benefited from having the realities of this very "mean business" shared with us early on in our careers. It would have made victories easier and defeats more understandable. And be forewarned that we intend to beat these realities into your head in as many different ways as we can. Like any politicians worth their salt, we know that you must present a consistent message over and over to the public until it sinks in.

1

★ ★

A CORPORATE APPROACH

THE BASIC RULES FOR ANY CAMPAIGN— FROM PRECINCT CAPTAIN TO PRESIDENT

Every business starts out with an idea, a product or service that the proprietor believes to be uniquely superior to anything previously offered the consumer. Every politician starts out with an idea, a belief that they can serve the public with a superior set of goals or talents the likes of which voters have never seen. Nine times out of ten, whether it's in business or politics, there is a huge amount of ego fueling the desire to enter the arena.

And ego isn't necessarily a bad thing. Without the self-confidence that ego provides, few political candidates would ever get their effort off the ground. The only bad thing about ego is when the candidate fails to recognize that it exists. As Congressman Johnny Isakson, the modest moderate who replaced Newt Gingrich in Congress, puts it, "It's hard to beg when you're not on your knees!"

So if you've decided you want to run for office (or you're the loved one or staffer of someone who does), the first question becomes: Where does a potential candidate start? The answer is very simple: By formulating a campaign plan.

It seems that everyone who refers to himself or herself as a "political consultant" places great value on the mysterious strategy known as "the campaign plan," as if it were somehow photocopied from the secret playbook of Vince Lombardi. In reality, most campaign plans supplied by even the most experienced professional consultants are basically cookie-cutter replicas of plans from other campaigns, involving little original thought.

This is not to underestimate the importance of the campaign plan. On the contrary, the creation of a truly effective campaign plan requires the same skills needed to write the score for a musical or choreograph the intricate movements of a ballet. Campaign plans must incorporate all the mundane organizational logistics, while at the same time capturing the long-term (at least as far as the campaign is concerned) strategic side of a political war. And, in reality, most who claim to understand how to lay out an effective campaign plan lack the true knowledge to do so at the optimal level. Don't be fooled. There is a straightforward, uncomplicated formula for these so-called "plans." Don't be worried if you do not yet understand all the following terms; you soon will.

★ Begin by listing your campaign's key supporters and forming a campaign committee (which we, in a very businesslike manner, like to refer to as "a corporate board"). This includes the creation of a fund-raising committee.

★ Start the process towards both image and issue development. This includes conducting an early benchmark poll to help your campaign define and refine key issues.

★ Begin creating a sequential timeline for your Internet presence, earned (free) media efforts, paid mailings, television/radio, and the all-crucial voter identification and GOTV (Get Out The Vote) effort.

★ Determine the essential staff for each segment of the campaign. For instance, the start-up phase will be skeletal with a few high-end paid staff, even in big statewide or national races. The race towards the primary (if there is one) will require either paid or volunteer staff to answer phones, handle any "in-house" mailings, manage the campaign Web site, deal with press, schedule events, organize fund-raising and fund-raising events.

★ Create the campaign budget, back-ending it from election day to the first day of start-up. Determine the amount of television, radio, direct mail, paid telephone "get-out-the-vote," and other contact with voters the candidate will need to adequately deliver both for the primary and general election victory. Figure each amount based on a schedule proportional to the size of the race: gubernatorial races often start with television as soon as the nominees are decided and don't stop until election day; smaller races often don't attract the attention of the public until two or three weeks before the election, so why waste money earlier? Factor in Internet costs, as well; the good news here is that your biggest expenditure is up-front, for site design and construction. (Don't hesitate to ask someone to volunteer this service.)

★ Finally, before the first consultant is hired or the first volunteer takes control, create that special "media account" where a certain percentage of all funds is placed under safekeeping. Have it guarded by a trusted supporter or relative of the candidate—and don't allow it to be spent until the campaign has reached the point at which direct contact with the voter is crucial (even if it means losing most of the paid staff or a major consultant).

To get some perspective on the world of politics, we turned to a political veteran, Newton Leroy "Newt" Gingrich, former Speaker of the House. An army brat whose true Southern roots are virtually nonexistent, Gingrich built his career as an outside backbencher lobbing political bombs in a skillfully strategic manner. He learned early on that a mixture of image and issues can result in success in the world of politics.

☆

Very few aspiring politicians realize the value of ideas. Certainly coming up with new ideas is not an easy task. But to creatively offer new solutions to age-old problems is the very essence of successful political and governmental advancement.

I remember in the early 1980s suggesting to the Reagan administration that they include a tax credit for every family that purchased a then virtually unknown and unheard-of item called the personal computer. My suggestion was politely, but firmly, 'blown off.' The same fate awaited my argument in favor of an international space station. While at the time those concepts might have seemed slightly goofy, the fact is that they did come to fruition. And the same can be said for many ideas that many bright individuals with whom I served in Congress on the Republican side helped create during the late 1970s, '80s and early '90s.

Grass roots are the true center of political growth. Building a strong grassroots network is critical to creating true change. But grass can only flourish with care and nurture. The lifeblood of grassroots growth is the power and energy of ideas.

Most political observers believe that the 'Contract with America' was the work of a handful of powerful GOP House members and a few consultants. Nothing could be further from the truth. In reality, the 'Contract' began with very small meetings of (then) very low-ranking minority members of the House and very bright, but relatively obscure, young strategists in the early 1980s.

We really did believe in the power of ideas. But those ideas required a great deal of fleshing out and faced the additional hurdle of being questioned by many within my own party's establishment.

So, I guess to put it succinctly, I am a great believer in having a well-thought-out message about which a candidate can not only speak passionately, but about which he or she feels equally excited.

Now, as for the concept of image, well, I guess there's little shock in the fact that I had greater difficulty in grasping the importance of this concept than one might have expected. Of course a great deal of the attacks one faces, at least as the first Republican Speaker since the 1950s, come with that highly unusual territory. But clearly there were issues of how we positioned and explained what I continue to believe to be strong and important legislation (particularly after the 'hundred days') that, in hindsight, could be revisited. My best advice on the question of image is not to let it be totally obscured by your message, your mission. That's not to say that you abandon your principles or give up on what you believe in—instead it is a recognition that the legislative or policy side of what you are saying has to ring true with the lifestyle and concerns of the people who will be voting.

As far as issues go, well, I believe there is strength in numbers. As a candidate (or elected official), do not be an island unto yourself. Find the very brightest colleagues or friends that you can and spend time listening and learning from them.

One of my closest friends once asked me why it was that when I would go to a fast-food place or a grocery store I would ask the cook or the person at the cash register endless questions about their job, how they performed it, how things could be made better. 'Why do you give a damn about how hamburgers are cooked, Newt?' my friend ribbed me. 'Because,' I replied, 'you never know when you might have to deal with issues related to meat quality or food services . . . or when you might be flipping hamburgers for a living!'

CREATING YOUR
BOARD OF DIRECTORS

Just like in most publicly held corporations, you will need to create an initial "board of directors" for any campaign for public office. A corporate board is often made up of "outside directors" who know little about the technicalities and nuances of the product or service that the corporation provides to the public. They are there for the experience they have gained in their own successful endeavors and for the prestige or connections that they bring to the corporation as board members. And, in most instances, corporate board members have some financial or personal interest in seeing the company do well.

Everyone who seeks public office has some type of base, such as friends, family, coworkers, fellow club members, etc. Before starting any campaign, gather up lists—handwritten or listed from membership rosters—of individuals you know from various civic organizations, clubs, churches, and companies. Examine your lists carefully and select a manageable number of individuals with whom you have a good relationship or, alternatively, whom you may not know but believe might be receptive to meeting you. Think of someone who has in the past supported candidates with your political ideology or agenda.

And, while both indirect and direct financial gain should never be a premise for someone seeking to participate in a political campaign, the reality is that the "inner circle" that makes up your "board of directors" will need to feel a real sense of accomplishment for having been chosen to be a member of your board. That way, they can feel good about themselves and any connections they might make, and really get "fired up" about your campaign.

Here are some helpful hints for making your "corporate board" a success:

First, make sure that you keep its numbers proportionately small. Statewide and congressional efforts need no more than twenty-five to thirty major directors. Smaller races need fewer than ten. Any larger a group makes the members seem as if they really aren't all that special and creates an unruly mob of outspoken leaders, often with divergent and politically naive opinions.

Second, let your "board of directors" give real input and have a true role in your campaign. Political consultants and campaign managers love to look down their collective noses at such volunteers. Of course it never dawns on them that these businessmen and women have somehow managed to earn and create more wealth, support more charities, and accomplish more personally than all of these so-called campaign "experts" could ever dream of doing. While we firmly believe that consultants, pollsters, and advertising experts are essential professionals who usually understand the "real business" far better than an insurance executive or accomplished attorney, they nevertheless need the reality check that your "corporate board" can

provide. And more importantly, your board needs to feel that its collective and individual voice matters. Otherwise, why waste their time
with another politician?

Finally, use your "board of directors" to help recruit other supporters who will form other groups within your campaign, such as the
larger "steering committee" or specific groups designed to attract key
demographic segments of the electorate. Having important civic and
business leaders listed as your "campaign cochairs" (or whatever term
you may choose for key "directors") will help attract the next tier of
potential supporter.

Think of the sales representative who has spent years trying to get
to know that key corporate vice-president, and suddenly finds his
entree as a member of the broader "steering committee" of your campaign. Make no mistake, many a significant business contact has been
established through political campaigns, and because campaigns tend
to be personal and tough, they often create a sense of camaraderie that
survives long after the final ballot is counted—win or lose. This fact
needs to be part of your sales pitch in attracting not only your key
"board" but also the foot soldiers who will make up your broader
steering committees, or groups such as "Veterans for . . . " or
"Businessmen and Businesswomen for . . . ". These groups will ultimately give you the level of participation necessary to broaden not
only your fund-raising efforts, but also the all-important "grassroots"
aspect of your campaign that Gingrich mentioned. They need to
believe in your message and need to want to share it with others.

FUNDING YOUR
POLITICAL IPO

One of the reasons that initial public offerings of corporate stocks (IPOs) did so well in the 1990s was because very few investment pros wanted to be left out of a business deal that might take off and rocket to success. And the same concept can often apply to a lesser-known candidate for public office. If people have a reason to believe in that candidate, they feel their investment (in time, money, or hopefully both) will not be wasted. Here are some basic rules for persuading individuals to become early or "initial" investors in your "public offering."

THREE RULES FOR ATTRACTING CAPITAL FOR YOUR POLITICAL IPO

1. Create a list of potential initial investors, then recruit these first investors to help expand the list.
Time is the enemy of any campaign because you are essentially

trying to create a workable and successful corporation in a much shorter period of time, and for a much shorter duration, than would ever be the case in the business world. Thus you must assemble your initial lists very quickly and begin to rate your potential "first calls" (those you will approach first for support). The name that pops up most frequently or with whom you have the best relationship should be the first person you ask to donate money to your campaign. And, assuming that he or she is a capable and respected person, this should be the man or woman who becomes your finance chairperson or, possibly, your campaign chairperson.

A word of warning: Many a candidate has early on named a campaign chairman or chairwoman only to find that a more qualified supporter emerges later with greater stature in the community or state. As egos enter into all phases of politics, the situation can quickly become tricky. Says one former candidate for a major office, "I started out with a person who had raised a great deal of money for various charities. This person was well respected for their ability to, as a volunteer, get people motivated to support the arts, as well as other civic projects. . . . What I didn't expect was that once this person agreed to become my campaign chair, he would completely abandon what he did best, raising money, and instead want to micromanage the campaign. Suddenly he was an expert about television commercials, issues, you name it. All of that diverted his time from raising money. My civic-minded fund-raising hero turned into a political monster. It was a disaster."

Our advice is to always leave room to insert someone at a higher level of your campaign. Thus, we suggest that your initial top "partner" be called the chairperson of the finance committee or chairperson of the campaign advisory board. If everything works out, this person can easily come to be known simply as the "chair" of your campaign, or campaign finance chair. If not, you can still make someone else the "campaign chairperson" or, if their political or financial status is of enough importance, you can name them "honorary campaign chairperson" or "honorary finance chairperson."

Regardless, you must create a list of fifteen to twenty individuals, along with an initial "chair" of that group, who will agree to contribute to, as well as raise money for, your campaign. If the campaign is congressional or statewide, then the commitment may well be for each person and his or her spouse to give one thousand dollars up front and to help raise another ten, twenty, or even fifty thousand dollars from others over the course of the campaign. For smaller races the amounts should, obviously, be smaller. But be careful not to "underprice" your IPO.

"The biggest mistake I ever made," says one member of Congress who ran unsuccessfully prior to being elected in 1992, "was to ask for too little. The businessmen I was calling were used to being asked to give the legal maximum. Oftentimes they would give a new candidate half or a third of what he asked for, primarily because they would be giving to two or three candidates in that same race. So when I asked for $500, they gave me 250 or even as little as 175. But when I asked for $2000, $1000 from them and another from their wife, then I suddenly found myself walking away with $1000 or, at the very least, the 500 I had thought I could never get during my first campaign."

The goal should be to get your committee of "initial investors" to help raise what would be approximately 10 percent of your full budget for the campaign. "But that's not nearly enough, and besides, I don't know what the budget should be," you might well be thinking. Don't worry about that now—concentrate on the fundamentals of asking. The rest we'll explain later.

What any candidate should really be wondering (and usually is paralyzed by the thought of) is "Why would anyone give me the first dime?" That leads us to . . .

2. Understand what your investor wants. . . .
Then try to offer a return on investment.

No two political "investors" are the same. One potential supporter may care passionately about a single issue, another may be more interested in advancing a particular image for their political party or community. Try to find out each potential supporter's interests before you talk to him or her. Then, if you find that you can or do—in good conscience—agree with their position or support their issue, approach each of them with zeal for their particular cause.

Always remember, however, that a return on investment should never include or even imply that some sort of financial or other unethical reward will be given when you are in office. That sort of conduct creates a slippery slope from which there can be no rescue.

Remember that the largest segment of political donors will be those who just want access, who want to have a personal relationship with someone they like and believe will "go places." Even the much-maligned Washington lobbyists know that with today's scrutiny, their donation guarantees them at best a chance to claim that they are "friends with the senator" or congressman. They sell that tenuous access, along with their insider knowledge of the old-boy system, to corporations that have no alternative but to hope and pray that their lobbyist can at least get their side of the story heard.

So the fact that you might be running for a seat on the local school board doesn't mean that a potential supporter might not believe that you're ultimately headed for the governor's mansion—or even the White House. You will find some people attracted to politics who will invest not in who you currently are or the job you presently seek—but who you might be and where you might be serving ten years down the road.

"Bill Clinton was the best I've ever seen at running for one office while clearly creating the impression that he was destined for much bigger things," says one political consultant who worked with Clinton during his early years. "His secret was that he acted like he was one of us, but carried himself as if he were already the president! That created a star quality for him, even when he was a struggling nobody."

There's a lesson to be learned there: people like a winner. But you don't always have to win to get their support; as a candidate you just have to carry yourself like a winner—speaking confidently, looking fresh, and never denying that you may well have "bigger fish to fry" down the road. But for the time being, you must make clear that the biggest fish to you is the person you're talking to at that very moment.

Indeed, most political writers and observers have remarked about having the same experience we did upon our brief separate encounters with President Clinton. Clinton has an almost surreal ability to make the person to whom he is speaking feel as if they are the most interesting and important person in the room. He avoids making the fatal mistake that 99 percent of other elected officials make—that of constantly glancing off to see who else is waiting to talk to them. Clinton obviously learned early on that you gain supporters and investors just like the advertisement says, "One at a Time."

3. Don't be afraid to "ask for the order."
Some of America's most successful CEOs constantly remind their sales forces not to be timid in selling their product. "Ask for the damn order" is the motto of one well-known head of a New York Stock Exchange company. If the thought of making a sales pitch about yourself turns your stomach, rest assured that you are not alone; many, if not most, candidates find fund-raising to be the most difficult part of running for office.

But here is a cold, hard fact that virtually every political candidate ultimately learns: no one can raise the money but you. So many candidates, particularly in larger races, search for professional fund-raisers who will somehow wave a magic wand and make the dollars flow in. The truth is that these "professionals" are, at best, facilitators. They can organize your systems, collect mailing or phone lists, and organize fund-raising meetings or events. They might even be able to collect a small amount of money based on personal relationships they have developed over the years with a handful of consistent big-dollar donors. But sooner or later (and usually it's sooner), the rubber meets the road and the candidate becomes the only "sales representative" who can "ask for the order" and get the donation.

The most essential element to successfully "asking for the order" is discipline. Just like in golf or tennis, only the players who practice on a daily basis are consistently able to win. Candidates for office must early on practice the art of asking for money. The initial solicitations should, as noted earlier, be for high-dollar participation and usually require personal meetings (breakfast, lunch, drinks, or a visit to the donor's home or office) to seal "the order." To help get used to making that first step (or first dive) into the freezing pool of fund-raising, the candidate should dip in his or her little toe by targeting one or two key donors with whom success seems likely.

But after these initial "easy hits," candidates must resign themselves to making endless phone calls and personal pitches for money. The secret to approaching this is to take your projected total budget (we'll discuss the budgeting process a little later), divide it by the number of working days between your campaign commencement and the general election (always assume a primary election victory!), then divide that number into 130 percent of your budgeted amount. Why 130 percent? Because studies show that almost every campaign runs 20 to 30 percent over budget.

The figure that this simple calculation produces is the amount of money that you, the candidate, must raise on a daily basis (yes, include weekend days to make the task seem a little more reasonable) in order to successfully capture a victory.

Remember how earlier we mentioned the fund-raising capabilities of the Internet? We'll expand on that topic even further in a later chapter dedicated solely to the Internet and political campaigns. But for now we just want to remind you again that no smart candidate should go into any race relying upon the Internet as his or her only mechanism for raising funds, no matter how excited people got in early 2000 when "outsider" candidate John McCain, a Republican senator from Arizona, raised literally millions of dollars "from" his Web site after winning the New Hampshire primary. There was a lot of work that went on *offline* to drive potential contributors to donate to McCain *online*. Yes, include the Internet in your arsenal of fund-raising tools. But remember that the candidate still has to do a lot of non-electronic "asking for the order."

And remember this, too: The candidate who raises the most money wins more than 90 percent of all contested races in America. A cruel fact, but true.

Perhaps no one understands better the dynamics of fund-raising than former Arkansas Senator Dale Bumpers. Bumpers may be best remembered recently as the man President Clinton asked to make his final defense argument before the U.S. Senate during Clinton's impeachment trial. Bumpers, a former governor of his home state, was elected to four terms in the Senate, choosing not to seek reelection in 1998 despite the conventional wisdom that said he would easily have retained his seat. He is presently affiliated with the Center for Defense Information, a Washington think tank focusing on defense issues.

☆

I must say that asking for money was the toughest thing I faced when I ran for governor the first time. I had no idea how important money was in a campaign, but I soon found out that I was going to have to start asking people for money. It was the toughest thing I ever did.

But you overcome the aversion to asking for money in two ways. Number one: Necessity, pure and simple. Number two: Simply getting used to it. In all my campaigns, maybe as many as fifteen campaigns I've waged since 1970, every time I came up for reelection and had to start raising money I would work my way into it. Success begins to put your aversion to asking in the background. You get on the phone and start calling people and you have a good day and then the next day is not nearly so difficult to face.

Of course television and the media are what is driving this mad, crazed necessity for money. You cannot wage a regional, a statewide, or in most instances even a citywide election campaign without tremendous television exposure, and that has just become increasingly expensive.

Now, money will subsume most other people. If you have a lot of money, a lot more than your opponent, the chances are that you are going to win. Statistics show that 94 percent of the candidates who spend the most money do win. That's one of the reasons we know that money has such an inordinate influence.

Should we limit campaign financing? I'm one of those few people, there are now maybe twenty or twenty-five in the United States Senate, who strongly favor public financing of campaigns. It has worked extremely well in presidential campaigns. I simply do not understand the aversion people have for it. I tell chamber-of-commerce types, all right, you like to play the market and sit around the coffee shop and talk about what a great investment you made. You couldn't make a greater investment than the few bucks you would spend financing campaigns and taking money totally out of the equation.

Realistically, you won't ever take money totally out, but you can render it virtually ineffective as far as policy is concerned. Right now, you see, money is not only necessary but it also drives public policy, and public policy usually ends up being what the big hitters say it ought to be. We've gotten to the point where it has become such a whoring proposition to run for office, and candidates just tell people what they think they want to hear.

SECRET TIPS OF EARLY FUND-RAISING

Now that we've covered the candidate's burden, and that of those convinced to participate in creating this "ongoing business," we should share a few logistical tips that make the fund-raising process easier. Some of these tips are simple. Others of them many presidential candidates have yet to learn, much less master.

1. Center your early efforts around one big event.

Campaign kickoffs are the perfect opportunity to test the viability of your "board" or "finance committee" (which, as stated earlier, may range from only a handful in small races to as many as thirty in statewide or congressional efforts), along with your much larger "steering committee" comprised of less involved but supportive individuals. These two groups should form the nucleus of your kickoff, or announcement fund-raiser.

Some candidates feel the need to lean on the crutch of having some other well-known business or political leader (or perhaps even a celebrity) be the "drawing card" for selling that initial fund-raising event. This is a mistake. Your campaign kickoff fund-raiser will be the one event that is likely to draw your true supporters and friends. Why waste a big-name draw such as a popular athlete or sympathetic political leader when you know that this core group will attend anyway?

It's much better for you to be the draw, because you are the candidate. The initial kickoff needs to prove that you are capable of raising a crowd—and money—on your own two feet, with the support of your host committee.

The key to the success of this first major event is setting the right donation price and establishing as large a group of members as possible who are willing to serve on your host committee. Most people will be more than happy to have their name appear on a printed invitation to the event. A few may ask not to appear on any list, and you should respect their wishes while still asking them to participate quietly.

The event should be sold on a ticket-by-ticket basis. And never set the amount of donation too low. This is a common mistake that many candidates, even for the highest offices, tend to make when creating their first major fund-raiser. The best way to determine what to charge is to ask a variety of people, including several veteran elected officials who have held fund-raisers in recent years, what they think is a reasonable ticket price.

Make sure that each host agrees to be responsible for, or to buy, a set number of tickets. For example, most gubernatorial races have campaign kickoff dinners or receptions where the sponsors are asked to sell ten, twenty, or even more tickets to the event at amounts of five hundred dollars per person or couple, one thousand dollars per person or couple, or more.

Never leave the amount of the contribution open to "whatever the donor might wish to give." That strategy, although polite, will never net a candidate as much initial money as will a set amount. Even if your ticket price is too high, many potential donors will give you a lesser donation and simply not attend. So keep in mind that the kickoff event is a general fund-raising tool as well as a venue to launch the campaign.

2. Keep fund-raising expenses to a minimum.

The biggest point that even the most sophisticated national campaigns often fail to recognize is that the amount of cash on hand to buy print or electronic media during the heat of the election is really much more important than how much money the candidate raises overall. If all of the money the candidate raises is going to pay for "professional fund-raising experts," staff, expensive invitations, or overpriced and unnecessary food and entertainment at fund-raising events, there will be little left at the end to purchase the weapons that are the most essential in winning a campaign.

Just like with a business, every department should operate within a budget, including the fund-raising arm of the campaign. Excluding the ongoing cost for staff (or a professional fund-raising expert) and invitations and postage, the actual out-of-pocket expenses related to any fund-raising event should always be between 10 and 15 percent of the realistic total expected to be raised at the event.

For example, in a smaller campaign, where the realistic goal to be raised at a fund-raiser is $5000, the total cost of the event location, food, drink, and entertainment should be somewhere between $500 and $750. Add an extra 2 or 3 percent to cover the cost of printing and postage, and the total cost of a well-run event should leave the candidate with almost 80 percent of his or her money safely stashed away in the campaign's bank account.

Such a lean budget may well seem impossible. But candidates should remember that many expenses they consider automatic, such as the rental of a facility, can often be eliminated by utilizing the home or office of a key supporter. And an expensive catering bill can often be eliminated in smaller campaigns—where the event price is less—by purchasing inexpensive party foods and limiting alcohol (if offered) to beer and wine, thus eliminating the need for a bartender. Remember: they don't come for the food!

All of this may sound like something out of a party-planning guide or cookbook, but a strict adherence to these rules will leave the candidate more money to spend on reaching the voter when that crucial time comes along. That is, if the candidate follows the third important tip . . .

3. Do not even consider hiring a "professional fund-raising expert" until after you have completed your campaign kickoff event.

The single greatest mistake candidates for everything from local sheriff to U.S. president make is to believe that they can hire someone else who will magically produce all of the funds the campaign needs, therefore freeing the candidate up "to concentrate on meeting the people and dealing with the issues." That scenario never develops. Any person who calls him or herself a "professional political fund-raiser," and in any way suggests that they can raise the money for the candidate, is simply a con artist. As we mentioned earlier, these so-called "experts," at the very most, can help organize the effort (including events), obtain mailing lists, assist in making direct mail solicitations for funds, and make follow-up calls to collect funds pledged to the campaign. But rarely do the contributors who gave to a consultant's last candidate automatically open their checkbook for the expert's next client.

We address the topic of hiring professionals and staff a little later on. Suffice it to say that a candidate for any campaign smaller than that of a major statewide race should attempt to raise their first funds by utilizing only volunteers and, at most, one paid event coordinator.

Once you've seen that you can raise money on your own, you will have the experience, confidence, and ability to decide exactly who and what you need in order to raise the many more dollars your campaign will need.

4. Use the telephone.

So many candidates are afraid to make their initial pitch for money in any setting other than a breakfast or lunch. This approach creates a myriad of problems. First, there is the difficulty of getting on the calendar of a busy businessperson. And in most instances there is a third party who is introducing the candidate to the potential donor, so there are three calendars that must match up. Such logistical hurdles can leave a campaign stuck in the mud before it ever gets off the ground.

We suggest that the telephone remains the best friend of the political candidate. Having staff and volunteers develop a strong and accurate potential donor list is of immense importance. But it is the candidate who must make the calls.

To help break the initial ice, obtain a phone that allows for three-way conferencing, and ask those who know the potential donors to join you in making those introductory calls. This is not to say that many potential fund-raiser hosts or finance committee members won't require meeting the candidate in person. But the calls will produce many who will agree to give without the need for protracted (and expensive) breakfasts or lunches, and those who do require additional meetings can be scheduled with the candidate and the common friend on the line at the same time.

5. Make your new friends and financial supporters
a part of your "board of directors."

Just as any initial public offering of stock or securities has its "ground floor investors," there is also the next tier of individuals who want to be a part of the start of something big. In the political arena, this tier is comprised of those the candidate meets or calls who decide that they are willing to invest a substantial (relative to the size of the campaign) amount toward the effort. These individuals should be offered a role in the campaign as well. Always be expanding your campaign's "official" structure by adding such individuals to a host or steering committee. People who participate in politics, just like in business, want to have a structure upon which they can rely. Generously supply titles and duties, and hold regular meetings to assure these individuals that they are not simply token members of the team. The more they feel like an integral part of your "corporation," the more likely they are to help secure additional dollars towards the end of the campaign, when funds will inevitably become tight.

The most successful national campaigns of the modern era have all taken a "no-nonsense" business approach. John F. Kennedy's 1960 presidential effort was a pure application of then-emerging high-level business practices to that era's far less sophisticated world of politics.

Money was raised by a true financier, JFK's father, Joseph Kennedy Sr. Permanent aircraft, phone banks, televised "specials," and commercials were all developed and utilized. Celebrities such as Frank Sinatra were used to "push the product," much like he was a dish detergent or an automobile.

The businesslike approach reached its apex when Richard Nixon, whom Kennedy defeated in 1960, made his successful bid for the presidency in 1968. Nixon's team applied the more sophisticated ploys of Madison Avenue to establish "the new Nixon." And the skills developed by the Nixon team were honed to a sharp edge by both the Reagan and Clinton campaigns. The Kennedy campaign began the "trickle down" effect that image and message would have not only on presidential campaigns, but on state and local political efforts as well.

Perhaps one of the greatest, and certainly the most recent, example of fund-raising prowess using the now-traditional corporate approach comes from the 2000 presidential campaign of Texas governor George W. Bush. Bush utilized the allure of being a former president's son, combined with his service as governor of one of America's biggest states, to capture early on the vast majority of the Republican Party's fund-raising machine. But he did it in a most methodical manner.

In the fall of 1998 and the winter/spring of 1999, Bush began a well-orchestrated series of small and intimate meetings. Key supporters from around the country would select a handful of GOP "movers and shakers" to fly, on private jets, for an afternoon or evening of "quiet time" with the governor. The Bush camp knew the Republican Party like the back of their hands. They knew that capturing the three or four key money people in each state would virtually guarantee a lock on funds through the primary season. And why?

First, Republicans often go with the perceived winner. Perhaps it's the slightly "nouveau" in them, or perhaps it's simply their good business sense. Regardless, getting a lock on a state's three or four big GOP donors early virtually guarantees that the many other potential donors, who follow like sheep, will also support that candidate.

Republicans love their "intraparty" establishment. And most second- and third-tier GOP donors will follow the lead of the established "big dogs." Bush, by courting those big dogs with private jets and personal dinners, locked down the Republican money elite before any other candidate could get to them. And it didn't hurt that he possessed the sort of outgoing, charismatic personality that could keep those big dogs "pumped up" during their flight home. It was only after Senator John McCain pulled off a New Hampshire upset that GOP donors began to hedge their bets.

A devotion to "the establishment" is not limited to the GOP. Al Gore's candidacy was fueled primarily by those who were insiders in the Clinton administration. But the more diverse makeup and more complicated "old-money" structure of the Democratic Party can allow a challenger with elected experience to raise sizable sums. Consider former senator Bill Bradley, who combined his popularity as a former professional athlete with certain key special-interest votes, such as his opposite stand from Clinton/Gore on issues of telecommunications reform, into big Democratic establishment support. That left Bradley with more in his coffers than those challenging the Republican front-runner in early 2000.

SECTION

★ *2* ★

"SHOW ME THE BUSINESS PLAN"

CREATING A CANDIDATE, A MESSAGE, AND A MARKETING PLAN

A campaign without a message is an empty shell doomed to failure. Likewise, a candidate who cannot clearly articulate the reason for running will never succeed. The most memorable example of the latter is the Roger Mudd interview with Senator Edward M. Kennedy about his candidacy for president in 1980. When asked why he wanted to be president, the normally articulate senator could not give a convincing answer. We believe that the candidate should develop early on a short and cogent statement as to why he or she is running. This statement should come from the heart and appeal to the better instincts of the electorate. If you can't say it in a few sentences go back to the drawing board, because no one will understand a rambling explanation of your candidacy.

The essential task of developing the message of the campaign must begin with an issues poll. Most issues polls point up the obvious: voters want better schools, safer streets, and a cleaner environment. But polls also contain valuable nuggets of information that are not so obvious—veins of discontent that can turn an election if the sentiments they reveal are consistent with the candidate's record and beliefs.

PIERRE: When we did our first poll in 1989, I had no less than 5 percent statewide name recognition after eighteen years in the state senate. We needed an issue. We found it deep within the cross-tabs, showing that older voters and their relatives wanted nursing home reform. Since I had chaired the senate committee dealing with these issues, nursing home reform was a natural for me. The nursing home owners were already for my opponent, so politically it made sense. It became a centerpiece of the campaign and enabled me to get to the vast majority of voters over fifty, the most reliable voters of all.

MATT: When I ran for lieutenant governor in 1990, I relied heavily on the message that it was time for a change. Georgia had never elected a Republican lieutenant governor, and the message resonated strongly with some voters. But I learned that your message must convey specifically what you plan to do in office to make life better for people. Things that people talk about around the supper table. Voters want to know what's in it for them.

SORTING OUT
THE IMAGE

Two basic rules govern the creation and communication of a candidate's public image and message:

Rule #1
Be realistic about your vulnerabilities.

As we have noted, politics, even at the local level, has lamentably become a blood sport. Too many candidates, in formulating their own images, fail to take into account the more vulnerable sides of their character, personality, and past. It would be wise for anyone considering a run for public office to learn whatever negative information his or her opponent might uncover long before the opposition even realizes you exist. Those running for reelection must go through this same process as well—sort of like an annual visit to the doctor for a checkup.

In low-budget races, there is likely to be little money available to engage professional assistance in accomplishing this sort of self-inflicted background check. In such cases it would be wise to find a local confidant, such as an attorney, public relations expert, or other trained professional, to make a search of available public information on you. Many times they can perform this task on a voluntary basis for little or no cost. High-dollar and/or larger campaigns should engage a qualified professional investigation company to perform this same background check. But they should first require the agency and its investigators to sign stringent nondisclosure agreements drafted by an attorney.

Candidates in small campaigns must then sit down and make a very blunt (and often painful) list of any and all potential past incidents that might somehow be discovered and exploited by less-than-scrupulous opponents. Divide your list into personal matters (relations with others, past romantic interests, marriages, divorces), qualification issues (education, professional, or job-related past), and finances (past loans, business partnerships, investments).

Make a list of every conceivable issue that might be raised in these areas, as well as any public information that your trusted supporter may have uncovered, and then begin the process of preparing a response to every conceivable last-minute accusation that could be made against you. Do not candy-coat your assessment. Be brutal in determining how your opponents might twist what appear to be innocent or explainable circumstances into scandals or attacks on your capabilities.

Make this list—including your answers—and share it with no one. Absolutely no one, not even your potential consultants or managers. Then take comfort in a basic fact: Most attacks of a personal nature are seen as "dirty campaigning" by the public and backfire on the candidate who employs them. The only time that last-minute attacks are generally successful is when there is an official record or a legal proceeding, past or current, that somehow gives the attack legitimacy.

Consider the true case of a candidate for a state legislative seat who was the essence of the squeaky clean "all-American." His opponent, utilizing a crafty campaign consultant, filed a last-minute ethics charge against him and then mailed copies of the articles reporting the charges to thousands of voters. The charges, flimsy and doubtful, were later dismissed, and the opponent was later publicly rebuked by the state's ethics review panel for filing such a weak and unsubstantiated set of allegations. But the "all-American" failed to recognize that the public will easily accept even the most fallacious of complaints if they are in the form of a legal action. He lost the race because he chose not to respond to his opponent's attack with flimsy ethics charges of his own. It spoke volumes about his character, but it also cost him the election.

Then there was the candidate who appeared to be a lock for winning his party's nomination for high office. A well-known consultant began to befriend this candidate. They had the ritualistic breakfast and lunch meetings where high-level candidates and potential consultants woo and measure each other. The consultant won the trust of the candidate and asked the question that many modern-day political strategists ask: "Do you have any potentially embarrassing problems from your past?" Thinking that he shared a professional relationship with the consultant, the candidate made a fatal error: he answered "yes" and proceeded to spill his guts to the consultant. But there was just one problem—the consultant had yet to sign a contract. He had no duty of confidentiality, at least from a legal standpoint, to the candidate. Months later the consultant had moved on to assist one of the candidate's chief opponents. Within days, the confidential secret was a raging rumor that tormented the poor candidate. In the end the secret was secret no more. The candidate was ruined.

The respected University of Virginia political science professor Larry Sabato reminds us that "the press is never more pious than when it is on 'sin patrol.'" So potential candidates should take stock of their "past sins" and be very careful about how or when they confess them.

Once the candidate has identified his or her weaknesses, the next task is to devise a campaign message that avoids turning the weaknesses into the most dreaded of all political sins: hypocrisy. Focus group after focus group teaches us the simple rule that the American public simply despises politicians who "throw rocks, but live in glass houses." That's why some of the most flamboyant, ill-mannered, even "ethically challenged" individuals have managed to get reelected time and again, while straitlaced leaders have been turned out of office for a single mistake. The public, as a general rule, will tolerate a great deal from its elected officials—but it won't tolerate a blatant hypocrite.

So the self-righteous religious zealot who, as it turns out, may have a DUI or drug charge in their past will do well to either admit early on to past mistakes, or to get off his or her high horse. No one wants to be labeled a political version of *Saturday Night Live*'s Church Lady!

Rule #2

Define yourself long before your opponents have a chance to define you in less flattering terms. Since name identification is the most important element for victory, make sure it's the identification you want.

Everyone wants to be loved. And often candidates for office fail to realistically assess the likelihood that the public will admire them as much as they admire themselves. There is the story of a wealthy businessman who had twice sought statewide public office, only to lose each time by a slim margin. Although intimates knew him to be a warm and loyal friend, his appearance and wealth gave him a cold persona the public never seemed to accept.

On his third effort—a second bid for governor—advisors suggested that he spend his millions early on, defining all potential opponents in the same unflattering manner in which they would later define him. Because he had run twice before, the candidate already enjoyed a huge name-recognition advantage over them. Had he chosen to spend his money six months earlier defining his opponents on television, before they had raised sufficient funds to reply, he could easily have left them all in the dust.

Instead he chose to wait. Running the same lackluster ads as his previous campaigns, he was too busy trying to make the public love something they had twice rejected. His opponents finally raised enough money to define themselves—in glowing and flattering terms. The result was predictable. The businessman, who seemed a cinch to win, garnered no more love or affection the third time around than in his prior attempts. He lost the general election. The sad part is that he really was a good and decent man. It was strategy, and unfortunate timing, that defeated him.

In most political races, he or she who has the strongest favorable name identification ends up the winner. And in races of lesser importance ("down-ballot races"), the candidate with the greatest name recognition, period—be it bad or good—will usually defeat other opponents.

Why? Because, like it or not, most people don't give a damn about politics or politicians. They focus on political races only days before the election, and even then it is a miracle if more than 50 percent of those who took the time to register actually go to the polls and cast a ballot. Even if they vote, some will do so only in the top "marquee" races, leaving less publicized races to be determined by the very few who are either informed or motivated.

This makes the early development of a candidate's image crucial. It also means that no matter how hard the candidate works to create and refine both image and issue positions, he or she will likely have many months during which that effort will appear to take place in a vacuum—with only a few months or weeks late in the process in which to project their image in a way that penetrates the public's lack of interest.

The number-one rule is to make sure that when the public finally begins paying attention to the race, your candidate is the first to take to the airwaves, mail the literature, and post the billboards which project the positive self-image that best portrays the campaign and his or her candidacy.

Listen to what others have to say about your appearance, voice, mannerisms, and reputation. Confront your weaknesses early on and make any necessary alterations, if possible. A recent example of such alteration can be found in Elizabeth Dole's early efforts at capturing the GOP nomination for the 2000 presidential race. Dole was well known by insiders as being "a control freak" who wanted everything well scripted and perfectly planned. The national press was already irritated with her prior to her campaign, because, as one national correspondent put it, "she's an ice queen." But by late summer of 1999, Elizabeth Dole had undergone, at the very least, a visual makeover. Gone was the perfectly 1970s hairstyle. Less frequent were her appearances in tailored suits draped with jewels. By the time of the Iowa straw poll in early August, Mrs. Dole had become a far more down-to-earth candidate—she had literally "let her hair down." Although she eventually withdrew from the race, Dole rallied impressive support among women voters, and positioned herself well as a strong potential candidate for the GOP vice-presidential nomination.

When determining image, it is always best to get the help of someone who makes his or her living in public relations or advertising. In a small or low-budget campaign, it is wise to seek out volunteers in those fields who can take the feedback from a "nonprofessional" focus group and evaluate how the candidate's image stacks up against the image the electorate has of itself and looks for in its elected officials.

In larger campaigns, there are scores of professional media trainers and advertising consultants who do nothing but craft images and issues for their candidates. Occasionally even the most sophisticated candidates (particularly those who have been around for a while and have tired of the usual techniques of traditional consultants) choose to "go outside the box" and hire a general advertising agency whose specialty is marketing cars, sodas, or cereal. We have seen this happen several times, but cannot recall many instances when these efforts have been successful. Why? Because despite the fact that many top political advertising consultants are retreading the same old material and seem stuck in the "inside the Beltway" rut, they at least understand the intricacies of big-time campaigns. They know how to read the cross-tabs of a poll; they've experienced that last-minute attack right before election day. Although they may seem to be arrogant bandits with spotty win-loss records, they are nevertheless specialists in the field. It normally takes a general public relations firm or advertising agency—no matter how large or respected—far too long to learn all of the nuances of a political campaign. By the time they have learned them, two things have happened. First, their candidate has lost. And second, their management has already vowed never to do another campaign.

Ultimately, each candidate must confront their own image on video, through the eyes and ears of others, and every time they look into a mirror . . . and then go about emphasizing their strengths, and try to shed or camouflage their weaknesses. Once the candidate has clearly established who he or she truly is, then attention must turn to what the campaign message will be. The candidate is the product that must be sold to the consumer, but every good businessman and woman knows that a product without a message simply won't sell.

CREATING
"THE MESSAGE" IN
BOTH BIG AND SMALL
CAMPAIGNS

Most elected officials are certain they know what the public needs and wants. If they have run in big-budget races before, they usually have experience with professional pollsters and consultants. But whether a candidate is a first-time county commission hopeful or a U.S. senator running for his or her fourth term, there is a simple formula that the campaign, in its early stages, can employ to save time and give more efficient direction to those who will craft polls or create focus groups. And all it takes is a careful count of newspaper and broadcast news stories. Here's how it works:

Go back four months from the date on which you are starting to formulate candidate positions on issues. Make a tally of the top ten news stories that concern the nature of the race (local, state, federal). The issue or story that appears most frequently in a combination of the leading paper's news and opinion sections should be assigned the number 1. Rank the remaining topics in descending order based on

frequency of appearance. Take the top five issues and begin an inten-
sive monitoring of leading television and radio broadcasts for three
weeks. Again, assign numbers in descending order to the most often
mentioned subjects on the broadcasts. At the end of three weeks, add
the scores of the top five newspaper topics to the top five broadcast
topics. The three that were mentioned the most are likely to be the
most important issues as the campaign commences.

Now take your three issues and begin the campaign's issue development process. The value of this approach for smaller or less expensive
campaigns is that it allows the candidate the opportunity to have a good
"ballpark" idea of what issues to focus on, thus saving time and resources.
It also can be important for the largest of campaigns. This simple formula can be carried out by volunteers and gives even a seasoned veteran
the ability to more accurately direct his pollsters, consultants, and
researchers towards those issues and topics that will resonate with voters. It saves valuable time and money that otherwise would be spent listening to consultants from another state telling the campaign staff and
candidate what questions should be on the first "benchmark" poll or
raised in the first "professional" focus group. Once the general issues and
topics that are most likely to motivate or concern the electorate have
been established, it's time for issues research and the development of
potential position papers.

In well-heeled or larger campaigns, issue research is usually conducted by staff members with strong research skills and a background
in general public policy. But in smaller budget efforts, or even big
statewide or congressional campaigns where the candidate is making
his or her first appearance, you will likely need to make initial issues
research and development a volunteer or low-paying "contract" job. In
such instances, the best place to start is with college students who are
majoring in political science, journalism, or history, or with a young
lawyer or other professional who is up on general current events.

The researcher should start with publications, public voting records or other public documents, as well as the Internet. After doing a strong search in these areas, they can turn to think tanks (such as the liberal Brookings Institution or conservative Heritage Foundation) or less partisan sources, such as the American Legislative Exchange or the Council of State Governments, for white papers and other policy reports in which new and innovative programs are discussed and analyzed.

While developing positions, candidates and their staff would be well served to remember that in politics there is no such thing as plagiarism—no one has a copyright on ideas. Just ask the Republicans, who in the mid and late 1990s saw Bill Clinton cherry-pick their very best ideas and make them part of his agenda. Was that wrong? No way. It's part of the business—an idea belongs only to the candidate who steals it and most effectively promotes it. The Republicans sat around yelling "foul" for Clinton's blatant appropriation of some of their ideas. And what drove GOP members even more to distraction was the fact that President Clinton often altered their programs so that they appeared to be the same, but lacked the more conservative GOP-crafted details. Too bad! Clinton remained popular despite an impeachment trial, while the GOP barely held onto its majority in the House and Senate.

Once issue research has begun, and the campaign has a good handle on both the problems and potential solutions, it's time to test these two elements with real voters. Professional campaign experts almost always use paid "professional" focus groups to help understand potential public reaction to potential television ads or responses to potential crises. But every campaign, be it for U.S. president or city council, needs to start with a basic focus-group discussion that springboards off its initial assessment of the issues that matter to the electorate, as well as the potential positions the candidate might take on those issues. The problem is that many campaigns either lack the money to conduct a professional focus group, or have the money but waste it by not conducting first an inexpensive but highly instructional informal focus group. Here's how an informal focus group works:

Ask your "corporate board" to recruit a few of their friends who are not involved with the campaign for an hour and a half of their time one evening. Each should state the purpose of the evening as "research for a cause that is important to me." But neither the campaign nor the candidate should ever be identified with the focus group. As a means of encouraging participation, small gifts, such as certificates for dinner or a drawing for an expense-paid weekend trip, can be offered. The participants should be made well aware that their participation and identity will be kept confidential.

Out of some thirty or forty people invited, you may well have only seven or eight who accept. But attempt to make sure that those who do accept at least broadly reflect the composition of the electorate whose vote you are seeking. In other words, if 55 percent of those who normally vote in the primary or general election are female, an all-male focus group will probably be counterproductive.

The focus group should be held at an office or hotel conference room where there is no chance of interruption. It should be conducted by an articulate and friendly leader who takes an objective approach and who carefully avoids dominating the conversation or steering it in a particular direction. If at all possible, the session should be videotaped, or at the very least, voice-recorded. The leader should always recognize the person speaking so that, in the replay, the listener can identify each participant.

The goal of any focus group is to gather words. Questions should be written out in advance and should concentrate on the issues reflected in the combined print/broadcast survey. Participants should be asked to give words and phrases that reflect their feelings, ideas, and solutions to various issues or problems that are raised. The leader should list the key words the group comes up with on large sheets of paper, so that they can be studied later.

Based on this step-by-step approach, a well-financed campaign can save a great deal of money and time by giving its professional staff and consultants a more directed target for their polling and research. A less well-funded campaign will now have a leg up on its opponents with regard to issue and image development. The results will hopefully help create an image combined with a message that reflects not only the issues the candidate believes in, but also those that will resonate with voters.

MERGING IMAGE AND
MESSAGE TO CREATE
THE FINAL PRODUCT

Once the issue positions have been created and the candidate has determined his or her best attributes and greatest strengths, there must be a merger of image and message. It's time to put together the whole package that will be presented to the public. For established candidates, this latest election might be a chance to retool their image or reveal new issues. For first-time candidates, this election is their opportunity to introduce themselves to the public. Without a well-established self-image, a strong message is lost and vice versa. And the candidate must feel confident in both areas.

Consider the fate of former vice president Dan Quayle. In 1988, then-vice president George Bush shocked the world when he chose a young, handsome senator from Indiana, J. Danforth Quayle, as his running mate. Within days of his selection, Quayle faced a barrage of questions concerning his membership in the Indiana National Guard during the Vietnam War. The Bush campaign made the situation worse by brutally and ineptly handling the young senator and treating him like a child. They basically told the stunned Quayle that he should stay quiet and follow orders. It was an unnecessary trauma that, in private, Quayle admits had a long-lasting effect on his self-confidence. And the lack of trust that this mishandling created within the campaign contributed to the uneasiness that replaced Quayle's normally relaxed and affable manner.

Bill Nigut, a television reporter who covered the 1988 presidential campaign:

☆

In 1988, and this was after the convention, we were traveling with Dan Quayle in Orlando. By this time Quayle had been relegated, by the Bush campaign, to making only two or three appearances a day, so it was fairly easy work for those of us in the media. So one afternoon, after we had covered some fairly insignificant event, we (the press) all commandeered a bus and went to Disney World. I don't recall if it was Jackie Judd (of ABC News) or who it was, but someone got the idea that, to break the ice with the Quayles, we would all buy those stupid Goofy hats, the ones with the long ears. So the next day when the Quayles came down from their hotel suite, we were all there wearing these hats.

We convinced P. F. Bentley (the famed photographer, then with Time magazine and noted for his somewhat stilted ability to get his words out) to present a hat to Dan Quayle. Sensing that it probably would be a mistake to don a silly hat, Quayle hesitated. But Marilyn didn't. She snatched the hat from Dan's hands and slapped it on as if to say, 'You thought you were going to make him look stupid, but I fooled you!' That was a shame, because it was meant to show our affection for him. Everyone really liked him. But they took a chance to turn bad press around with humor, and blew it.

Quayle's humor didn't emerge until years later, and the destruction of his self-confidence turned the bright and articulate young senator into a halting, stumbling, and sheepish vice president. After years away from those who had treated him as a "political child," Quayle regained his old self-confidence, humor, and ability to hold his own in an interview or debate. But the damage had already been done.

The lesson of Dan Quayle is one that every campaign manager and consultant would do well to consider. Even the brightest rising political star can be extinguished with too much control or criticism. Creating a candidate with the proper image and message prior to unleashing him or her on the public will not only allow for a smoother and more attractive campaign effort, it will also provide the candidate with the most essential element of all: confidence.

Whether the race is a major national contest or a local slugfest, here are basic rules that will help guide the creation of "the final product." These rules should be followed before attempting to write the speech that the candidate will give over and over again during the later stages of the campaign.

1. Create three basic talking points, and always bring every conversation back to these three issues, no matter what the question might be.

Remember those top three issues that emerged from the combined news surveys and "informal focus group"? While a larger campaign may have honed in on its issues through a more professional route, the end result of any campaign should still boil down to the top three issues that each candidate believes will resonate with the particular electorate needed for victory.

To keep these issues in the forefront of their mind at all times, the candidate must first generate concise but specific lines that describe each problem as it currently exists, why this problem is of importance to the voter, and the candidate's solution—and nothing more. The candidate should be forced to practice these lines, first alone, and then later with staff or close supporters. And no matter how tough the first questions from the media or potential voters might be, the candidate should always steer the conversation back to the issue (of their chosen three) that seems the most relevant to each question.

If a question has no obvious connection to any of the three issues, then the candidate should go back to the most important issue and stick to it. This is called "redirection," and although this tactic falls under our later discussion of "advanced techniques," it is the most fundamental method of doing what every candidate must do: Stay on message. We'll talk more about the concept of the three issues when we cover campaign speeches in chapter 6.

2. Never discuss an issue or take a position until the candidate and his or her advisors have carefully researched and considered the facts and implications.

We both remember moments during our respective campaigns when we "popped off" a quick answer to a potential voter or to a reporter's question that seemed to come flying at us out of left field! Take it from us when we implore candidates and campaigns to remember the art of redirection by politely noting that "this is a very important concern that we need to explore thoroughly"—then quickly returning to one of those three comfortable central issues. The candidate should always promise to get back to the questioner, but should never comment on a matter about which they have little familiarity or on which he or she has failed to determine a position. In this type of circumstance, the less said the better.

3. As the campaign advances, drop issues that are no longer relevant or aren't working and substitute them with well-researched new issues. But continue to keep the arsenal limited to three.

No one can stand to hear a candidate say the exact same thing month after month. This makes it important for candidates for every possible office to rotate new issues or ideas into that reliable repertoire of three major issues. But the changes should be done one at a time, and the candidate should not substitute a new position or idea for an existing one until he or she is completely familiar with, and has practiced articulating, the new issue.

And a special word to candidates: We all have issues about which we feel passionate. Realize that if you get elected (or reelected), you will have the ability to take on those matters with all of the zeal and attention you want. But if an issue is one that doesn't seem to motivate voters, drop it from your core set of topics. Better to select winning ideas for your "central three" issues; leave your pet projects for after the election.

4. Voters are impressed with facts and examples. Give them both.

It's amazing how many experienced national candidates who, wanting to be vague in their early positions on issues, fail to recognize the simple trick of deflecting attention from a weak positi-- solution by offering a strong description of the --- a candidate's three issues, he o--- facts (numbers a--

5. Remember that too many cooks in the kitchen spoil the broth. Come to a consensus among the key members of your "corporate board" and "management team," then ignore the unsolicited input you receive from outsiders.

There is nothing more destructive to creating a centralized image and message than for the candidate or staff to change that message every time someone expresses a different opinion. That's not to say that a campaign and its candidate should ignore overwhelming public reaction to a part of their message that clearly isn't working; if the candidate hears constant criticism about tactics or positions, gather the "inner circle" and employ the same techniques used earlier (or a quick poll or focus group) to determine if there should be an immediate change in direction.

But in general, candidates who follow the sort of methodical approach we've set forth should have confidence in their research process and should ignore the day-to-day comments of "armchair political advisors." Listen politely, tell them that you value their opinion and will consider it, and then move on, doing exactly what the campaign has collectively set in motion as its image and message plan. In most campaigns, the candidate who sticks with a well-set strategic plan and resists second-guessing wins the election. In other words, a consistent image, message, and plan—even a mediocre one—often triumph over a brilliant candidacy that never remains consistent and is constantly in turmoil.

When determining the direction of your campaign strategy, it is _____ that there are many statistics available on the _____ this new millen-

years. Candidates in all fifty states should find the following data highly valuable.

Men continue to be more likely than women to vote Republican. Prior to 1994, the percentage of men who voted Republican had been three to six points higher than that of females. In 1994, the difference soared to eleven percentage points; in 1996 it was nine. In the '98 election there was a seven-point gap between the number of men and women who voted Republican. Potential candidates will also be interested to learn that the voting differences between men and women are even more evident among voters with college degrees and voters under the age of thirty.

In the last three elections, the *New York Times*-commissioned survey found a majority of voters sixty and older gave their votes to Republican candidates, perhaps signaling the departure of the Democratic-leaning New Deal generation. This trend is seen among both sexes, although it does not hold true along racial lines. Sixty percent of older white people voted for the GOP candidate in their district, but older black voters continue to overwhelmingly vote Democratic.

In terms of party loyalty, the Republicans have been doing a better job of holding onto most self-identified GOP voters, getting at least 90 percent of their votes. Democrats have also been doing well at retaining their base vote.

An interesting trend is that for the past three elections, increasing numbers of independents—who make up a little more than one-fourth of all voters—have been voting Republican. In 1998, the votes of independent women were equally divided between Republicans and Democrats. Independent men, in general, are more inclined than independent women to vote Republican, but not to the degree that they were in 1994. Also, a majority of white voters who consider themselves independent voted for the Republican candidate. And although a large majority of black independents supported the Democratic candidate, one-fifth favored the GOP standard-bearer. This general trend was manifested in John McCain's strong appeal to independents in his race for the GOP nomination.

As expected, financial concerns still dominate the minds of most American voters. And voters appear to turn against the incumbent party when they believe their economic situation has worsened. Democratic candidates in 1998 were favored by those voters who believed their situation had improved under incumbent president Bill Clinton. Most of the voters who described their family as being either less well off or the same voted for Republican candidates in 1998, as they had in 1996 and 1994. In 1980, 1994 and 1996, Democrats were backed by a majority of voters who felt their financial status had improved.

The *Times* survey found there are still some signs of the social alliances that have existed since the Depression era. For example, less affluent voters—those with an annual income of less than thirty thousand dollars—gave the majority of their votes to the Democrats. Black, Hispanic, and Jewish voters remained strongly Democratic, as did urban voters and households with a union member. By contrast, white Protestants and voters whose income exceeded thirty thousand dollars tended to vote Republican. GOP candidates were favored by suburbanites, as well as by those who live in small towns and rural areas.

In the end, all the research, demographic information and realistic assessments of available resources—both financial and human—should be assimilated into the creation of the campaign strategy. But here is a crucial piece of advice: Every campaign plan, whether written by a rookie volunteer or one of the top consultants in America, must contain something new—some idea, concept, or logistical twist—that has never been seen in the ward, district, or state in which the candidate seeks election. More than anything, it is uniqueness that the American electorate seems to embrace. Just like us, they've seen it all. So be sure to give them at least one thing they haven't yet experienced. It may well make the difference between victory and defeat.

THE
CAMPAIGN SPEECH

Once the key issues have been identified and the message is close to being developed, it's time to create the basic campaign speech that the candidate will rely on like a crutch. Look at these speeches as an opportunity and not as a burden. In fact, they are just what any candidate should be thankful for: a chance to stand before voters—and the media, if you're lucky—and state your case. For a few precious minutes, you have everyone's undivided attention (or at least their respectful silence) and, unlike the process of spreading your message by direct mail, broadcast commercials, or handouts at the mall, speeches don't cost you a dime. So take advantage of this great opportunity by taking the time to think about exactly what you want to say, and then saying it briefly, simply, and clearly. Beyond that, it's mainly a matter of nerve.

There's the rub, of course; most of us are afraid, or at least a little uneasy, about speaking to a crowd in a formal setting. If you're not afraid, you're already halfway home. Your confidence is going to be apparent in every word and gesture, and the only thing you have to worry about is making sure your positions are clear (and popular), and that your self-confidence doesn't come across as arrogance.

For the rest of us, there's a certain amount of anxiety involved. If you count yourself among this humble majority, take heart, because most people in the audience are paying scant attention to the proceedings anyway. And even if they listen to your every word, they're probably going to forget them in about ten minutes. Abraham Lincoln once said, "The world will little note, nor long remember, what we say here today." (This was true of just about everyone's speeches except his own!)

But relax, the situation is not as discouraging as we've made it sound. Even speeches before the poorest of listeners are an important political ritual, like campaign bumper stickers and qualifying fees. And political rituals are like other rituals—everyone thinks they're important even as they ignore the particulars. For example, consider the social ritual of singing the national anthem at ball games. If it goes as routine dictates, the crowd forgets about it as soon as they sit back down. Why? Because it is a social custom, something that's always done and puts people at ease. Nobody gets goose bumps at the thought of bombs bursting in air. But if the national anthem is left out of the proceedings, watch out—like most rituals, it is only noteworthy in its absence.

Giving a speech is oddly similar. If it's routine stuff and is going well, the audience will react by feeling comfortable that political obligations are being met. Then they're likely to smile and tune out. But don't despair, because they're also warming up to you as someone who's toeing the line and paying his dues. They'll remember you even if they don't recall your words. They'll leave the building with an impression, even if they can't verbalize it. But they don't have to verbalize it—all they have to do is punch your name on the ballot.

Audiences understand the rules. They know it's a game, and if you play by the rules, you will earn their approval. You may play the role well or play it poorly, but "play" is the operative word. In fact, even if you break out in hives and stutter uncontrollably, the audience is still going to note your self-destruction with clinical detachment. It's like spotting roadkill on the highway. Maybe you sympathize and maybe you could care less, but either way you're just going to swerve around the wreckage and hit the gas. Remember that your audience is more concerned with the rest of their day than they are with your political fortunes. So relax.

The first step is to write a standard speech you can use over and over. Don't worry about the same people hearing the same message at future events—people need to be told again and again. When a voter steps into the voting booth, he's not going to hold discourse with himself; he's going to vote on a general impression (those voting along strictly philosophical or partisan lines are often beyond the reach of persuasion anyway). Remember those key issues that the campaign identified early on? Select the three most important, and build your basic speech around them.

You can and should, of course, make minor modifications to your standard speech, based on whom you're speaking to and what the occasion is. You might change the order of presentation or add one new item if you think some in the audience might have heard you before, but, as we've mentioned, voters want consistency in your views. If you keep changing them in an effort to be interesting, voters figure you're going to be just as fickle once you're elected. You're not running for an Academy Award, you're running for public office. So hammer home your points. If your policies are the right ones, they bear repeating.

Be sure to write out the speech in detail. If you memorize it, all the better. But writing out your ideas forces you to clarify them.

The more passionate you are about an issue and the longer you've held that view, the more likely it is that your opinion has become second nature. And what's second nature is not easily articulated. Spell it out—literally. No, the audience is not going to boo or stomp out of the room if your speech is muddled. Their unspoken reaction will be much more basic and damaging. They will simply tune out and think about something else. Worse, they will probably vote for somebody else.

Write your first draft at least a week before you speak. When you go back days later and re-read it, you will discover many things, not the least being that many passages that seemed red hot have turned to cold ashes. Conversely, other passages that you scribbled with hardly a thought will suddenly leap out at you as if someone else—someone brilliant and polished—had written them.

So, as we mentioned earlier, repeat yourself as we're doing here. Don't overestimate your audience. You may think a fact is universally known or a point of logic is obvious, but you can be sure that someone in the audience isn't going to get it. Besides, people hold a bewildering variety of worldviews, many of them frighteningly uninformed. Rest assured that someone is going to misconstrue your point if you let them. So say it again, and then say it one more time.

KEEP IT SIMPLE

Nothing is a bigger key to a good speech than this seemingly obvious point. When you sit down to write, forget about large audiences full of strangers. Just imagine that a close friend or family member is asking you what you plan to do if elected. Why in the world are you running for office, they ask? Write down your answer. Be brutally honest. You can always go back and soften the language or delete what's controversial. The best speech language comes as much from the heart as from the head.

When selecting your issues, speak not only about those that are proven winners, but also on something that you feel passionate about. A good example of the power of verbal passion is found in the "letters to the editor" sections of daily newspapers. Newspaper editors have been known to complain that letters to the editor are often better written than articles by seasoned writers. Why? Because people who write letters to the editor aren't getting paid for their time, and they aren't trying to fill up space. They're writing because they feel strongly about something, and they want to make their point with heat and without fanfare. The result? Eloquence.

You're looking for eloquence and energy in your speech. The only way to do that is to say what you mean and mean what you say. If you don't, it's going to show. Use simple language; it tells your audience that you respect them, that you've got nothing to hide. Plus, it gives them the impression that the solution to the problem at hand is also simple. The reverse holds just as true: If you smother the audience with flowery language, clunky rhythms, and faulty logic, they're going to see you as pompous and unqualified, and the issue as undefined and beyond your grasp.

In the art of language—from lyric poetry to bathroom graffiti to the president's State of the Union speech—less is more. That means short words are better than long ones. Instead of saying "We need to accelerate economic growth," say "We need to speed up economic growth." Don't use big words to show off. A great strength of the English language is that you can always find a different way of saying something. Find the simplest way.

"Less is more" also means short sentences are better than long ones. Instead of telling a group of bankers that "Interest rates are making it difficult for consumers and businesses to obtain capital," say

"Money is tight." Short, punchy sentences will lend your remarks a sense of movement and direction.

Finally, "less is more" means keep your speech short. Ten minutes is enough for most occasions. Twenty-five minutes is almost always too long. At the end of an hour-long talk, you could tell an audience that you're going to legalize assault and they would probably smile and start applauding. No one's paying attention. Don't bother wondering why this is—leave that to rhetoric professors and neuroscientists. Just believe it.

Unhappily, it's often the long-winded speakers who are the most celebrated. That's probably because no one has the guts to tell them to stifle themselves. Newt Gingrich is a good example. This former college professor has a lot of brilliant ideas. But he always seems to forget that his audience isn't a college class that's feverishly writing down his every word. The result is that by the end of his normal 45-minute lecture, most of the audience is reading the labels on their soda cans. No amount of steel-trap logic, polished rhetoric, or natural wit can overcome the God-given attention span of a banquet luncheon crowd. (But we should note that Gingrich today commands a fifty-thousand-dollar speaker's fee, so maybe keeping those speeches shorter isn't always such good advice!)

Just as a matter of self-defense, we'd like to ask what anyone remembers from President Clinton's marathon State of the Union speech in January 1999? Little if anything, we'll bet. What most people remember is the one subject he didn't mention: his own scandals.

It's true that orators of yesteryear were known to speak sometimes for hours, but speeches in pre-broadcast media days were cultural events, and rare ones at that. If the president of the United States was speaking to a gathering of farmers in the nineteenth century, you can bet that most of the people there had never before seen anyone so famous. To them it was more fun than a beach vacation. They were in no hurry to get back home and stare at the hearth.

Not today. People now are impatient and hurried. They've got more to entertain them than you and your words can possibly compete with. Say your piece and be done with it.

THE "BIG THREE" FORMULA FOR SUCCESSFUL SPEECHES

Keep the structure of your speeches simple as well. People remember things best in sequences of threes. The reason probably went to the grave with Aristotle, but never mind. Your speeches should be based upon the standard formula of "The Big Threes." First of all, have three basic parts to your speech:

INTRODUCTION: Here's where you offer an introductory joke or humorous anecdote to break the ice, as well as a few words acknowledging the specific group to whom you are speaking and any special friends or important guests who need to be mentioned. Note: self-deprecating humor is always safe. Make jokes that are short and punchy. Never make jokes that will lose votes. If you can get the audience to laugh with you, half the battle is won.

> **MATT:** Here's a classic example. A little girl wrote to me about my campaign for lieutenant governor. The letter said, "Dear Mr. Towery, We are studying state government at my school. Could you write me and let me know whether there is anything lower than a lieutenant governor?"

THE "THREE ISSUE" BODY OF THE SPEECH: This is where the "big threes" really come into play. You should discuss the three key issues that are most important to you, the candidate. With each issue, you should also use a three-pronged approach: 1) Identify the problem or issue and provide statistics or a story to illustrate it. 2) Provide a description of your proposed solution to the problem. 3) Give examples of what this proposed solution will bring about (if it's been tried in other states, then cite statistics or other evidence of its effectiveness).

CONCLUSION: A standard rallying cry that ties your three issues and your proposed solutions together so that the audience is left with a feeling that this candidate "really does have his or her act together."

This may all sound like numerology, but it works. Think in threes, and your audience is more likely to remember what you say. But on the flip side, don't get too carried away with the formal structure of your written material. First of all, even if you compose an outline that would make an English teacher proud—every point supported by a subpoint 'A' and 'B,' and so on—you'll never be able to deliver the speech with such flawless symmetry. Nor should you want to. Yes, speeches should unfold in an orderly fashion. But they should also seem natural, like conversation. If you speak by numbers, you're going to distance yourself from the audience. You're not a policy robot, you're a person. Speak like it.

THE SPECIAL SPEECH

Of course there will be times when the candidate will want to focus on a single issue. Those occasions call for something known as "the special speech." Speaking about just one topic virtually guarantees that even the most jaded listener will walk away with at least a vague impression of what you're about. Organize a special speech with the same basic three-part format as the "Big Three" speech, only dedicate the meat of the speech to a single issue. (But this does not mean you should forget about organizing subpoints and examples under that topic in groups of three!) A one-issue speech allows you to detail a particular point in a way you cannot do with your usual speech. This is a good approach if there's a hot-button issue a particular audience is excited about. Plus, using a special speech lends the air of a policy announcement to what you say, as though you are just making a position known for the first time. This can increase your chances of getting press coverage.

DELIVERING THE SPEECH: TO THINE OWNSELF BE TRUE

Instead of concentrating on formal principles of rhetoric, think more about just being yourself. This can be as hard to put into practice as it is easy to say. It's natural to want to be better than your self-image. Too many speakers, especially beginners, try to be more exciting, witty, or learned than they are. It won't work. Audiences are like children and dogs; they can smell a phony.

So how do you go about "being yourself"? By listening to someone else. It's best for this someone else to be a spouse, personal friend, or long-time associate whom you trust. (A speechwriter is ideal, but more on that shortly.) Have this person read your text, watch your closed-door rehearsal, and then attend the actual speech. Then ask them a simple question: did I come across as myself, or like a summer stock actor playing the part of a crooked alderman?

This point leads to the question of gender and style. If you're a woman, be a woman. Many women seek to suppress their feminine side because they're afraid of being seen as too soft. Don't do it. You've got to be yourself. Don't offer a football analogy if you hate sports, no matter how many Neanderthals are listening. Don't say you're going to "stick to your guns" if you faint at the sight of a water pistol. And if you speak more naturally by association than by a rigid line of logic, more power to you.

This is stereotyping, yes, but the point is valid. Obviously, the same principle of being true to your hormones also applies to men. But men aren't new to the political arena, so they're less likely to feel pressure to conform to standards of style they're not comfortable with. And men should remember that most voters are women. Remember: women typically don't vote for the Terminator.

It all goes back to having a message, articulating it ahead of time, and delivering it with the natural conviction that comes from truly believing it. Remember that the goal is to get elected. If you win your race, then presumably you're going to be expected to pursue the policies you promoted in your campaign. If you want people to listen to you later, don't melt them with hot air now. Consider the weight of what you're saying. No one would remember that President Reagan called the old Soviet Union "the Evil Empire" if he hadn't put Pershing missiles in Germany. After his deeds matched his words, you can bet that most people—including world adversaries—started paying more attention to Reagan's foreign policy speeches.

Humor is another tricky tactic. Humor in a speech should come like a thief in the night—unexpectedly. If you launch into a structured joke, you are raising expectations. That's okay if you know the joke is funny. But nothing makes an audience more uncomfortable than a speaker who expects them to laugh at something that isn't funny. Try out your joke ahead of time. If three different people spontaneously burst into laughter, go for it. Otherwise, drop it.

The best jokes are not really jokes per se, but humorous asides that color whatever serious point is being made. This kind of humor sneaks up on people, loosens them up in spite of themselves, and makes them more receptive. And if it doesn't work, it makes little difference because you haven't broken the rhythm of your speech. You can just bluff your way on to the next passage.

Self-deprecation is the surest way to get a laugh. People instinctively like people who can make fun of themselves. This is also a good way to deal with any embarrassing or hostile items about you in the press. When you acknowledge some unflattering public information about yourself, you drain it of its mystique.

The great rule of humor is that there are no rules, except just this one: Be funny. If you're in doubt, or you don't have the ability to cover a flat joke by making fun of yourself, take our advice and leave it out.

Of course, the style and message of some speakers isn't cut out for humor. They are more likely to read a profound quotation they've unearthed at the library. Quotations are fine only if they are relevant to your message and your audience—which makes appropriate ones hard to find. Quotations relevant to your subject are often boring, and those that leap off the page often don't support the point you're trying to make.

If you use a quotation, make sure it's worded in everyday language. Forget coffee-table books full of lofty pronouncements from people long dead. If you're going to quote Caesar Augustus, you might as well do it in the original Latin for all your audience will understand or care. Most old quotations are pompous and sterile, so avoid them. It's far better to refer to what a television character said last night, or what you read in the paper this morning, even if it's just the weather.

The use of irony is even more of a no-no. Irony is simply saying the opposite of what you mean as a way of emphasis. Irony saturates our culture, usually in the form of sarcasm: You tell your husband the gas bill is twice as high as last month, and he says, "Oh, great!" He's not really happy the bill is higher; he's just expressing his frustration in a creative and emphatic way.

Unless you are supremely confident in yourself and your audience, avoid irony. It depends too heavily on two things: subtle expression and an attentive audience with a high IQ. Though your listeners may be both, it's best to assume they are neither.

Besides, irony often comes across inaccurately when others, particularly news writers, repeat your words. An audience may howl with laughter when you tell them you don't support fixing the local school's air conditioner because kids need to learn to "take the heat." But when the speech is printed in the next day's paper and read by the humorless mother of six preschoolers, the only thing she's going to think is funny is your chances of getting elected.

Okay. If you're tired of hearing what you shouldn't do in a speech, here's something that's a good idea. Follow up your formal remarks with a question-and-answer period. It shows that you are receptive to the concerns of voters, and that you are comfortable with yourself and your beliefs. It also makes the audience feel smart. Those in the crowd who talk the loudest are also the ones most likely to keep talking when they hit the street. If you indulge their vanity, they might just talk about you.

Be careful when talking about topics with which you are unfamiliar or uncomfortable. The tendency in these situations is to fudge your words in an effort not to get it wrong. The result is that you end up talking without saying anything, or saying something you don't mean. The best solution? Study the issues.

Don't worry about hecklers and hostile questions; they're rare. Most people who don't like you aren't going to show up. If somebody does get nasty, turn it to your advantage. Show them all the respect they aren't showing you. Don't be afraid to disagree with them and defend your ideas. Most hostile questions come from people recognized by their friends as nuts. By simply outclassing them, you make them look adolescent and yourself mature. Above all, keep cool. Righteous anger is for advanced speakers.

By the same token, many speakers try too hard not to appear negative. Yes, you want to be upbeat and optimistic with voters, but not to the point of being a happy ditz. If you don't think anything is wrong with the policies of your opponent, maybe you should drop out of the race and vote for her. Unless you're running for kindergarten class president, tell it like it is. Respect will follow.

Another basic point that too many people overlook is to research the event at which you're going to speak. Assume nothing. Make sure, absolutely sure, that you or one of your staff phones ahead of time to find out about the layout of the room, the size and political mindset of the audience, the program agenda, the list of VIPs, the availability of good lighting and a microphone, etc. We have had to make speeches in every conceivable adverse condition: in a warehouse with no heat in mid-winter when the cold made you tremble; in hotel rooms next to a mariachi band blaring; in a cavernous auditorium without a microphone.

PIERRE: Once, as I was introduced to speak to a chamber of commerce banquet, I was hit with a severe nosebleed. Be prepared for anything!

Ask if the event sponsors have invited any media. It's better if they call the media, because it appears less manipulative than if you or your staff does it. That said, don't take anything for granted. If you have the slightest doubt, phone the media yourself. Better yet, fax them a press release and then phone them.

It's also a good idea to give the press some bait that will tempt them to come, and don't be vague about it. Tell them you're going to address some controversial issue. Of course where there's bait, there's also bait and switch. A speaker can always minimize the expected controversy when the time comes by talking only briefly about the promised hot topic.

Don't try to tailor a sound bite for the cameras. Television editors can cut tape to make you say anything they want. It's not that they necessarily want to make you look bad. They just want to air something that's newsworthy. The best way to provide just that is to deliver a meaningful speech with a consistent message to a receptive crowd— and a large one at that! Again, don't forget to post such speeches on your Web site. Do this for the benefit of both your supporters who want to know what you're saying when they can't be there to hear you, and your potential supporters who want to learn more about you.

Speaking of media, don't try any multimedia tricks yourself. Stay away from slide shows during your speech, unless they have a real purpose. Too many people are familiar with slide-show computer programs to be impressed by your fledgling skills. The only time slide presentations make a deep impression is when they go wrong. Speeches should be about words and ideas. If your audience wants entertainment, they're going to go to a movie instead of a political rally. Stick to the basics.

A word of warning: When you speak, always assume that what you say will be in the newspaper. That mousy little man in the back of the room may be a reporter.

If all these do's and don'ts are cluttering up your brain, you might want to consider hiring a speechwriter so someone else can worry about the writing while you concentrate on other things. This is a perfectly acceptable option, if your campaign can afford it. We will discuss speechwriters at length in Section Three.

Above all, the speaker (and/or the speechwriter) should learn to crave criticism. It's natural to avoid criticism and it's easy to create an environment where no one will tell you if your speech is faulty. If you encourage them not to say anything negative to you, they won't—but they won't say anything particularly positive about you to others, either. Remember that vision is drastically reduced when your head is buried in the sand. Don't just tolerate creative suggestions, insist on them.

Don't let too many people review your speech. Writing by committee doesn't work. The various egos will cause each reader to make changes just to be putting their stamp on it. The end result? A disjointed mess. Keep proofreaders to a minimum—one or two sharp and trusted people are sufficient—and leave the major changes to the one giving the speech.

Using secretaries as proofreaders can also backfire. They are prone to edit all material as if it is a business letter. They'll take out the contractions, sentence fragments, and other ungrammatical constructions that actually bring the spoken word to life. Speeches aren't grammar lessons. Don't treat them that way.

If you're still not convinced that you can give an effective speech, do one of three things. First, talk about the one issue that really gnaws at you. You've probably turned this issue over and over in your mind so many times that you could make your case to a deaf man. Put your passion to good use.

The second approach is to do just the opposite. Talk in clichés. Say what's been said before and proven to be safe. You may not win many votes, but you won't put your foot in your mouth either. If you can't use the occasion to move your campaign forward, at least don't set yourself back.

The third way to overcome fear of public speaking is also the simplest. Write it out word-for-word ahead of time, then read the damn thing. Many speakers think it's some sort of badge of dishonor or incompetence to read a speech word-for-word. It isn't. Many a seasoned veteran reads his speeches. We've seen governors who insisted on always having written remarks and were considered great speakers. They might be better at eye contact than you, but so what? If your message counts for anything, then the text of your speech is the important thing. Treat it that way. Just make sure the words are big enough for you to see easily. If that means you've got a wheelbarrow full of paper, so be it. It's certainly better than going up on the podium and hyperventilating from anxiety.

The surest sign of speechmaking success is when your audience concentrates on the content of your speech instead of its delivery. That way, they're not mentally coaching you through the speech, or rooting for you to make it to the end. They're not conscious that "here's a joke," or "this is supposed to be an applause line." If you have something to say and you say it with simple conviction, then the next time you stand before a crowd may be at your inauguration.

3

★ 3 ★

"SHOW ME THE TALENT"
TO EXECUTE THE BUSINESS PLAN

MERGING THE MESSAGE WITH PEOPLE

In the legal profession, there is an old saying: "The lawyer who represents himself has a fool for a client." The same could be said of a candidate who tries to run his or her own campaign. No football team would play in the Super Bowl without a coach; even the greatest quarterbacks realize they are too close to the action to make sound judgments—they rely upon their coaches to call the plays. Likewise, a candidate is too personally involved in the campaign to make sound decisions alone. A common refrain in losing campaigns is that the candidate "just wouldn't listen." While the candidate must have the final say and make decisions guided by conscience and belief, a winning candidate puts together a skilled campaign team and then heeds their advice. The winning team should consist of the following essential people: (1) a campaign manager; (2) a press secretary; (3) a media consultant; (4) a pollster; (5) a direct mail expert; (6) a speechwriter, if you can afford one; (7) a scheduler; and a few smaller positions such as a lawyer and CPA. In low-budget races, many of these duties may be consolidated and carried out by volunteers.

Before we talk about specific positions within a campaign, we thought it would be a good idea to consider the relationship between campaign talent and message selection. So we went to the master.

Robert Strauss has been the insider's insider in national Democratic politics for more than four decades, advising presidents from John Kennedy to Bill Clinton, not to mention fellow Texan Lyndon Johnson. He has served as chairman of the Democratic National Committee and Anti-Inflation Czar and International Trade Representative (under Carter). Republican George Bush tapped Strauss to serve as American ambassador to Russia. Strauss's law firm, Akin & Gump, is one of the most successful and influential in Washington.

☆

Putting together the staff and consultants is a vital part of any campaign. You have to look for people who have personalities and cultures you are comfortable with and who you can relate to. It has to be somebody you already know or someone you spend some time with beforehand. Be sure they have the right kind of recommendations and that you want to have them around you. I've got lawyers in this firm I don't want to come into my office. It isn't that they aren't good lawyers. They are very good lawyers or they wouldn't be here, but I don't particularly like their style.

I think body language, things like that, you have to have a feel about. I have a theory that the reason people are uncomfortable with Al Gore is that he's uncomfortable with himself. It shows in his body language. He never looks comfortable. Therefore, when I look at him, I'm uncomfortable for him. So I don't like to look at him. The same man has run my business for thirty years, better than I could. The point is, you better have somebody in a campaign you are comfortable with when it gets rough.

That's the first thing. Then you have got to have talent to tell the story you have made up your mind to tell, the strategy for that campaign, your reason for running, why you think you want to hold office. Make up a reason if you don't have one, something besides just wanting to hold office, which is the only reason a lot of these assholes have. You've got to have people who can tell that story effectively. If you are going to run a negative campaign, you want people who understand that sort of stuff.

You have to find your issues, take your issues, and relate them to what the public wants, what will sell. There is no point in spending a lot of money on advertising if you are not offering something folks like. There's an old story I always tell. This manufacturer of dog food keeps changing ad agencies, one firm after another, trying to sell this dog food. Finally, this little guy comes in and tells him, "I've done a poll of my own and I can tell you, you don't need to keep shifting ad agencies. You've got one basic problem: the dogs don't like your food." So there's no point in spending money on advertising unless you have a message. You've got to have a message the public wants to hear, that appeals to them.

I think the Kennedy campaign to capture the Democratic nomination was probably the best campaign I have ever seen. They had a lot to overcome and they really did it well. The Catholic issue hurt him in the South at that time. He dealt with that in his speech to Protestant ministers about their concerns. It was in Houston, Texas, after he won the nomination and Lyndon Johnson called down and told the guy who planned the event, "Put the meanest, bigoted-looking sons of bitches on the front row. I want these television cameras to show them, see those faces and then see the face of this fine young man we are running for president." That's a true story.

Michael Dukakis had the world's worst campaign. I think he didn't understand what he was doing. Different people would call me during the campaign,

*politically savvy people, and say, "I can't get through to him." It was too bad
because I liked Dukakis. I thought he would have been a pretty good president.*

As Strauss suggests, there must be a solid "business relationship"
and bond of trust between the candidate and the staff in order to run
a cohesive campaign. If not, it becomes much more difficult for a candidate to pull the pieces of the campaign together and to communicate
the message effectively to voters.

THE IMPORTANCE
OF A
CAMPAIGN MANAGER

In any successful campaign, the candidate must accept his or her proper role from the outset. Because most people who seek public office are by nature self-confident, energetic individuals, they often think they can run the whole show. This attitude is the quickest path out of politics. If the candidate is doing his or her job properly, he or she can't run the campaign—they simply won't have time. Running the campaign is the job of the campaign manager. The candidate must spend 75 percent of his or her time throughout the campaign on the telephone raising money. The other 25 percent is spent getting out the message of the campaign, in the manner and at the time and place designated by the campaign manager.

Gone are the days of wandering aimlessly from town to town, shaking hands at the courthouse and coffee shop. Any candidate activity that does not generate news coverage or raise money is wasted effort. There are many examples of talented candidates who have held public office and spent years making speeches throughout their state only to find that the first poll showed their name recognition in single digits!

A young state senator who had ambitions to run for statewide office once proudly told a colleague about a speech he had scheduled some four hours' drive from the state Capitol. The puzzled colleague asked the young senator why he would agree to do such a thing. "Let me tell you something," said the colleague. "Suppose that there are fifty folks at the speech. Forty percent of them aren't members of your party, so most of them won't vote for you based on party. That leaves around thirty potential votes. Half of the thirty won't agree with a damned word you say, so they won't vote for you. That leaves fifteen potential votes. Half of the fifteen, let's say seven, will forget you within six months, and won't recognize your name, so that leaves eight potential votes. Of the eight, two will die before the election, two will move out of state, and one will be declared legally insane. That leaves three potential votes. Of the three, one will be on vacation on election day and one will forget to vote. That leaves one potential vote. And you had better send him a birthday card or he'll leave you. You're better off having lunch with one person who can contribute a thousand dollars to your campaign. If you can't do that, just save your gas." The colleague who gave that advice is now a U.S. senator and the ambitious young state senator is out of politics. A good campaign manager could have told that young politician how better to spend his precious time.

The campaign manager directs the research into the candidate's record and that of his or her opponents. In addition, the campaign manager works with the pollster to develop the campaign message based on an analysis of the poll results. When the message of the campaign is established, it is the job of the campaign manager to keep the candidate "on message" and to minimize distractions. Almost as important, the campaign manager directs the staff to make sure that day-to-day details are attended to: a campaign office and

Web site must be set up; telephones and fax machines must be put in; news stories and television coverage must be reviewed daily; and myriad other tasks must be performed. No one person can attend to these matters and simultaneously function effectively as a candidate. The bottom line is this: Get the best campaign manager you can find.

Congressman Joe Scarborough is a rising GOP star who is outspoken about the lessons he has learned in the world of elections. He shares with us his very frank advice about selecting and working with campaign managers.

☆

In 1993, I traveled to Washington, D.C., to attend a Republican campaign management school. Through the course of the one-week program, I learned the basics required by a campaign manager to run an effective campaign. The only problem was that I wasn't the campaign manager, I was the candidate. The lead teacher at the school had warned me that I was such a "control freak" that I would have trouble finding a campaign manager to work with. Time proved him right.

As months passed, I searched for a suitable manager and always came away from interviews disappointed. In retrospect, I had unusually high expectations. However, I did come to learn what are the critical elements of an effective campaign manager. They include:

1. Loyalty
This may be hard to gauge, but if you can get it, you can leave the office worrying about shaking hands instead of watching your back. Who wants some clown questioning every move so he can take the credit for victory, while disavowing any missteps that could lead you to the losing column?

2. *Organization*

A campaign manager must make the trains run on time. For challengers running uphill, a campaign must look professional and efficient. Having no room for errors, a campaign manager must efficiently manage chaos every day. A good manager can make the most of the chaos. A great manager thrives on it.

3. *Friendship*

It helps if you like the manager and have a personal relationship with him or her. Long hours, high stress, rapidly changing conditions, and mood swings that are the norm in a political campaign can quickly erode a purely business relationship. Additionally, a campaign manager often has to play the role of cheerleader, counselor, punching bag, butler, and even devil's advocate. A manager can't effectively play all of those roles unless he or she is a true friend. However, always remember that the way you are fighting together is serious business. You must do what it takes to win, and your manager/friend must remember that you (as the candidate) ultimately call the shots. Your decisions are singularly focused on winning elections, not friendship.

4. *Attitude and Drive*

Campaign manager is not a job for someone who doesn't have a fire in the belly. Monetary compensation is not enough to make someone do a job that is often compared to herding cats for eighteen hours a day. Similarly, a manager with a poor attitude will bring down the whole team and send morale down the chute. If the manager doesn't believe in you, send him packing. Maybe he's right. Maybe you are a goober with no chance of winning. Even so, his lousy attitude will only make matters worse.

In the end, success is up to you. You the candidate must know what you want. Share this desire with your staff and your team and let it fuel the train to victory.

P. S. One sexist conclusion I've drawn: When in doubt, hire a woman. If you want someone to talk about how to get things done, go to a man. If you want someone to actually do them, hire a highly motivated woman—their egos usually occupy less space in cramped campaign headquarters. I know such generalizations are dangerous, but this one has always guided me to victory.

HOW TO FIND A CAMPAIGN MANAGER

Since James Carville and Mary Matalin attracted attention as opposing campaign managers (for Bill Clinton and George Bush) who later married, the public has become aware that there are people who make a living by managing political campaigns. Most of them start out at a young age working for a candidate under the direction of a pro. They work long hours and do the grunt work of the campaign. They also absorb everything, learning as much from mistakes and defeats as from brilliance and victory. At some point, these young turks get their big chance to run a statewide campaign. If they are successful, their reputations as winners quickly spread.

There are two strategies for selecting a campaign manager. The first is to obtain the names of managers for the most recent winners from your party in your state or district. Among these names are often some who are well known and command high fees, including a bonus for winning. It is also a good idea to go beyond your own backyard to get some names from other states.

The second strategy is to look for someone who is currently an assistant campaign manager, but who is hungry to make a name for himself or herself. The advantage of this strategy is that you often get the full attention of your manager, whereas it is not uncommon for the big names to run several campaigns simultaneously in different states.

When a campaign manager begins to spread herself or himself too thin, the product can suffer.

It is customary for the candidate to offer an expenses-paid interview to each prospective campaign manager. It is wise to have an initial tele-conference with prospective candidates for the job prior to incurring travel expenses to save time and money. Spend as much time as possible talking to them to determine their philosophy of running a campaign and to assure compatibility. Nothing is worse than being stuck with a campaign manager you just plain don't like.

THE IMPORTANCE OF
A PRESS SECRETARY

Dealing with the media is probably the most time-consuming and perplexing aspect of running for office. Whether talking to a cub reporter for the local weekly or a major national journalist, the candidate must be well versed in how to handle the uncomfortable situations that inevitably arise when politicians and the press corps mix.

In smaller campaigns, as noted earlier, a volunteer or a person filling numerous roles might have to take on the duties of dealing with the press. But there is one golden rule that no candidate should ever break: Never be your own press spokesperson. No matter how media-savvy a candidate is, no matter how well the candidate thinks he or she gets along with journalists, sooner or later there will come that time when the questions will get tough, the "friendships" will melt away, and in the heat of the battle you will say the wrong thing! Trust us, it happens to every elected official or candidate at one time or another.

Ronald Reagan was lucky enough to find his savvy press secretary, Lyn Nofzinger, during his 1966 campaign for the California governorship. Almost thirty-five years later, Nofzinger is still out there dispensing media advice to candidates. "In politics," he says, paraphrasing Leo Durocher, "with rare exceptions, nice guys finish second, which is good enough to lose." He also quips that "Losers don't legislate. They don't govern, either, nor do they redistrict or appoint judges. The list is long regarding what political losers don't do." What Nofzinger is saying is that in most cases, the candidate (or his surrogate or his media allies) will have to put a black hat on the opponent or opponents—and try to do it early in the campaign. Lee Atwater called it "driving up your opponent's negatives before you go positive."

Republicans, especially, have to fight hard to set the record straight with the great mass of voters because—let's face it—most surveys have shown reporters tend to vote Democratic and consider themselves more on the liberal side. Most claim to be objective, but some are definitely sympathetic to Democratic causes. Their news stories can be subtly or blatantly slanted, or they may even omit things from stories that might benefit the Republican candidate.

Incumbents often receive the same treatment, even when they are Democrats. There must be some unspoken desire in the heart of many journalists to see the underdog win. Besides, rooting for the underdog makes an otherwise boring race more interesting to cover. How many newsrooms across America wanted to see Bill Bradley give Al Gore a tough race, or see John McCain challenge the seemingly endless money supply of George W. Bush?

Sometimes reporters will "miss" a candidate's side of a public policy debate, and that candidate must then take immediate action. Don't let twenty-four to forty-eight hours pass before responding in some fashion to the other side's attack (or to a newspaper's critical omission). This is where the Internet as a communications tool can prove to be one of the most important weapons in your arsenal; the same communication you send out on this issue to the press can be simultaneously e-mailed to your supporters at no extra cost and posted on your Web site for future reference—and to clear up possible future misunderstandings.

SOME BASIC RULES THAT CANDIDATES AND PRESS SPOKESPEOPLE HAVE SHARED

Rule No. 1
Don't be afraid of journalists.

Rule No. 2
Be honest with reporters.

Rule No. 3
Keep it concise; don't say too much.

One of our favorite and most colorful friends in public office stresses the honesty dictum. "It's easier to remember the truth than a lie because journalists are writing it down or they are going to have it on tape. Regardless of whether you wish you could take a statement back, you can't."

He also recommends that "there's a time to shut up" when talking to journalists: "They ask a question; give them a truthful answer and that's it. You don't get into this long debate with them because they're always writing. And what was once a nice, concise answer could turn into twenty minutes' worth of rattling on. Then you could look foolish or it might look like you didn't answer the question. Get to the point quickly. Their job is to pull information out of you. Your job is to answer truthfully and concisely. Don't debate with them, because you're not going to win."

His last bit of sage advice? "When you're tired of giving answers, repeat the same answer over again. They'll get the point that you're not going to say anything else. And that's the end of the interview."

Remember, of course, that whenever you are talking to a journalist, the assumption is that the conversation is "on the record." Be sure to tell them when you expand on a sensitive point that it is "off the record"—and make sure the journalist verbally agrees. Silence doesn't mean he has agreed, so don't think that it does.

Playing favorites with journalists can be tricky. Generally, serve all of them out of the same spoon. If a press secretary writes a news release for the media on a major speech the candidate is giving, have the same embargo date on all the releases. Sometimes a press secretary might want to leak opposition research to a journalist (preferably a friendly one). Or the campaign manager or press secretary might want to promise a newspaper some "exclusive," especially if it is to a reporter or editor who is not warming to your candidacy.

If a candidate is being unfairly treated by a journalist, he or she should try to talk it over with the journalist first. If that fails, there is the option of complaining to the supervising editor or even to the publisher of the newspaper or periodical. If that fails, supporters might write a letter to the editor blasting the reporter (this can be risky), or the campaign might cut the reporter off from all campaign news. A new reporter will sometimes be assigned if a paper finds itself getting "scooped" by its competitors on your campaign.

If a terrible case of journalistic prejudice develops, always remember that newspapers, magazines, and electronic news organizations are all commercial entities, not authorized government investigators. A candidate doesn't have to cooperate or give an interview just to help make some commercial enterprise a little more money. If it's not beneficial, don't talk!

Can the media be prejudiced? Yes. Can a candidate receive fair treatment from the media? Yes. A candidate might even be surprised to find that a majority of reporters (especially outside of big cities) are basically apolitical, often in their twenties or thirties, and just trying to do a fair job of informing the public about the candidates. Candidates should always be polite and tell them they read their stories or editorials. It's the press secretary, or spokesperson, who has to be able to deal with the tough side of the media, the mean tricks of the trade.

Jody Powell is one of the best ever at understanding how "big-league" political journalism works. Part of Jimmy Carter's staff since his days as Georgia governor, Powell became a national figure while serving as Carter's presidential press secretary and advisor. "Never before has an American presidential press secretary wielded such power," the *New York Times* once commented. Powell now lives in Washington, D.C., and has his own public relations firm. He has written a syndicated column, has been a commentator for ABC News, and is the author of the book *The Other Side of the Story*.

☆

There are a million media tricks that a candidate or his campaign spokesman may encounter. One of the most common is if a journalist thinks you have information you don't want to divulge, he might call with some exaggerated report. It's a common thing. "Look," they will say, "I'm hearing so and so," and then give you some outlandish and terribly damaging sort of thing, which they threaten to write or broadcast unless you tell them the facts—which are not nearly as bad as what they are saying, though they may not be good. In your younger years, you quickly volunteer an answer of the not-so-bad. As years go by, you learn to try first to assess if they really do have something and if they also have it firmly enough so that they have the guts to report it. It may not really be confirmed and they are trying to get it out of you.

Example: They may say, "I hear you guys only raised X thousands of dollars last quarter," which you know is outrageous because the figure given is way below what you did raise. But the truth is you didn't have that good a quarter either, which they suspect. So, by threatening you with something much worse, they are trying to get you to divulge something you don't want to divulge on any basis.

Or, as another example, the journalist says, "I hear you have a poll that shows you dropped ten points." Well, you do have a poll and it shows you dropped five points. You don't want to reveal that, but you have to make a judgment. Are they going to go with the ten points if you don't admit to the five-point drop? You can always say, "I can assure you that what you say is absolutely not true, but I am not going to tell you what the actual number is."

It's a judgment call, sometimes a real risk. They know you don't want to tell them, that's not a big surprise. And they probably know there is no particular reason why you ought to tell them. It is not like you are failing to divulge something the public has a great right to know.

Dealing with a media crisis in a campaign depends usually on the nature of the crisis. The first thing in a media crisis is just to get all over it, find out everything you can as to what the facts are. There is no way for you to deal effectively with the media unless you know what the facts are yourself. Sometimes that can be a real challenge, because the information usually is not all in the hands of one person. Who said what, who did what. And, once things get into a mess, you run into a situation where everybody wants to cover their behinds.

I think probably the biggest media crisis we ran into in the Carter campaigns was on the Sunday before the general election in 1976. A black man, reasonably well known, showed up at the Plains Baptist Church and was turned away. As it turned out, it was something the Republican National Committee had put him up to, but here we were that Sunday, the polls that weekend showing for the first time that Carter and President Ford were dead even in the popular vote, then you have this thing that explodes on a Sunday afternoon.

One of the reasons it backfired on them was that a woman named Betty Rainwater was working there in the office in Atlanta that day, keeping track of everything, as you try to do, and she noticed that a statement from the Republican National Committee about the incident moved across the wire before the actual story moved across the wire. We did point that out to reporters. Of course, then many of our strong supporters, Andy Young and a whole lot of other folks, came out to California and appeared with Carter the next day. Actually, it ended up probably increasing black turnout, and I thought also it probably helped us with white Southerners, who viewed it as the typical sort of thing somebody tries to do to a Southern candidate, make him seem a racist no matter what his record is.

There is a problem in judging how good a campaign is, unless you are involved in it directly. If you are close enough to it, you see all the warts and mistakes, and you don't necessarily see that in other campaigns. Ranking them all together, I thought the first and second Reagan campaigns and the first and second Clinton campaigns were extremely good, extremely well handled.

Dealing with campaign financing is hard, also damned complicated. I have a view that it is worth drastically changing the rules on a regular basis, if for no other reason that it takes people a while to figure out how to get around them. If all else fails, just confuse it. Change the rules so people will have to figure out new loopholes.

There is a desperate human need to impose some order on any chaotic situation, when there may be no order there, including in political campaigns. My longtime observation is that any time you have a choice of betting on a conspiracy theory of history or the screw-up theory of history, bet on the screw-up. You will usually be right.

A campaign manager and candidate should also politely cultivate key media opinion molders other than beat reporters. There should be a personal meeting, or even lunches, with a newspaper editorial-page editor or political columnist, radio talk-show hosts, assignment editors, general managers, and commentators. Even if they don't always agree with your message, perhaps the candidate can charm them or just simply "give them tips."

A candidate must make sure newspapers, online media outlets, radio stations, and TV stations have a press kit that includes a photograph. With a daily newspaper, give the press kit not only to the political editor or reporter, but also remember the editorial page. The opinion page is a separate newspaper department—perhaps an even more important one than the newsroom. The editor in charge of the editorial page oversees the writing of opinions on your campaign, and also controls the widely read "letters to the editor" column. Many of these columns print letters focusing on a candidate and a related public policy issue. A campaign manager should get a few "readers" (i.e., campaign volunteers) to send in such letters, pointing out important points your campaign is trying to make (but don't deluge a paper with dozens of them). Keep them concise, and hopefully you'll get one or two published.

A news release, preferably faxed and/or e-mailed to a media outlet, should be used to tout a new public policy position or to answer an opponent's attack. A candidate shouldn't be angry if a reporter doesn't write about every release. Sometimes there are wrap-ups at the end of a campaign, and a reporter, editorial writer, or TV anchor might use quotes from a two-month-old press release. Be sure that there is a telephone number and contact (usually the press secretary) on the release, especially since a reporter may need a number to call quickly if there's a pressing deadline. Having such press releases posted on your campaign Web site, a technique we've mentioned before, is extremely helpful to reporters who might not have the time to play telephone tag with your overworked press secretary, but can take a minute or so to do some Internet research.

While we're on the subject of deadlines, it's worth noting how the advent of online media outlets—both those that exist only online and those that are cyberspace versions of their print and electronic brothers and sisters—have changed the deadline process. In the "old" days, a well-organized campaign knew that it had to release any information it wanted on the evening news and in the next day's papers by three o'clock. Now news can be released—and made—round the clock. And the pressure on reporters is greater: If news breaks, they no longer have the luxury of a day or even hours to be the first with the story; sometimes it's a matter of minutes between a speech or event and the time the first news report on it is available online to quite literally the entire world.

To best understand the mindset of the media, one must listen to experts who are an integral part of it. We asked a well-known political journalist to share with potential campaigns a view "from the other side."

Eleanor Clift has covered presidential campaigns and the White House for *Newsweek* and is currently a contributing editor. She has also covered Congress and is a regular panelist on the syndicated television talk show *The McLaughlin Group*. Clift and her husband, Tom Brazaitis, Washington columnist for the *Cleveland Plain Dealer*, are coauthors of the book *War Without Bloodshed: The Art of Politics* and the forthcoming *Madam President*, on the rise of women in American politics.

☆

From my perspective, from the media perspective, we love candidates who are candid or at least give the appearance of candor, so Senator John McCain was a real favorite this time around in the 2000 presidential campaign. He cusses and says things that can get him in trouble and you feel like you are getting a real person. Whereas the candidates who come across like robots are less admired. I guess Elizabeth Dole would clearly be in that category on the Republican side and probably Al Gore on the Democratic side—careful, cautious, never saying anything that should be off the record.

But what I'm saying is that what pleases the media isn't necessarily what works. The candidates who learn how to keep their mouths shut, who are disciplined—and George W. Bush is in that category, too—generally are more successful. The media loves candidates who don't pander, but the public doesn't always feel the same way, seeming sometimes uneasy with candidates who take positions that seem bold.

Senator Gary Hart's challenge to the press, "Come follow me," falls into a different category . . . setting a standard that you can't live up to, and that's a big mistake. Jimmy Carter did the same thing, saying "I will never tell a lie," so everybody was scrutinizing him on that basis. Remember? Somebody did an article, "Jimmy Carter's Pathetic Little Lies." Setting unrealistic standards . . . that's a mistake.

Playing the media's game is also a mistake. Following the media's timetable, for example. I think of Vice President Al Gore. He moved up his presidential announcement to the early part of the summer of '99. I don't think anybody was paying attention. Senator Bill Bradley had the discipline to wait until Labor Day.

Former Vice President Dan Quayle probably had one of the sorriest campaign experiences with the media. His big mistake was freezing up when he was asked about his military service. He had served in the National Guard and his service was certainly defensible, though there was an allegation that he used family influence to get in. But he panicked when he was asked about it and the media immediately sensed blood. I don't think he ever climbed out of that hole, though there were of course other issues he didn't seem to have a command of when put on the spot.

The media is unfair in the sense that it is always out of proportion. The media always piles on, because there are so many of us. So I think, in the end, the media is unfair because the person who is trying to explain what really happened can never reduce it to a sound bite.

Mistakes with campaigns always play a role. I am thinking of Jimmy Carter and his phrase "ethnic purity." He never could explain it and it sounded like racist buzz words. I remember Pat Buchanan, after he won the New Hampshire primary and then went out and immediately held that M-16 rifle or something similar over his head—which called attention to concerns people had about him, as opposed to allaying those concerns.

There was the famous photo of Michael Dukakis in the tank. People said he looked more like Snoopy than John Wayne, and I think that was unfair. But that photo op was planned by his campaign. The lesson for candidates might be, Be careful when you go in for props and gimmicks. That was a staged event. I remember another thing that was actually planned: Gary Hart's presidential announcement, when he went to the top of some lonely mountain . . . which just underscored the fact that he was a little on the weird side, not a regular guy. A lot of thought was given to that too, I believe. His campaign wanted to show the Western motif but instead they did not send the message they intended.

George W. Bush's presidential campaign in the early going may be the best I have ever seen. He's raised huge amounts of money. He seems to have been able to avoid totally offending the right wing of his party, though that may still happen. He has managed to seize the media's imagination. He is almost running as Myth, in a way I have never seen another candidate manage. A warm, fuzzy personality who seems just to have taken hold of the media imagination. The 1992 Clinton campaign was good, and it gave us a glimpse of the resilience that marks the more admirable side of Clinton's character. Resilience and focus. And then Carter's 1976 campaign was excellent in terms of relating to the country's pulse. His 1980 campaign was terrible.

The biggest problem the candidate has when communicating with the public is to seem authentic. Somehow, often, they don't seem genuine. Like Lamar Alexander running as a conservative in a plaid shirt, when his record was as a progressive, "New South" governor and a secretary of education promoting Goals 2000.

So, somehow, candidates have to be true to themselves. Somehow, they have to find a way to express who they are.

HOW TO FIND A GOOD PRESS SECRETARY

When selecting a press spokesperson or "press secretary," a campaign should search for someone with strong writing and verbal skills who can remain friendly even when seething mad, and who can handle the pressures that come with twenty phone calls, one after another, in the span of thirty minutes. After a campaign has found such a perfect animal, it's in great shape. Unfortunately, there are few individuals who truly meet that description.

Finding a good press secretary begins with finding two qualities in the person: 1) someone the candidate trusts and 2) someone who thinks like the candidate. Jimmy Carter chose Jody Powell, a young man from middle Georgia who began by driving Carter around the state in a race for governor. Powell was so close to Carter that he was practically a member of the family. Their relationship was one of total trust and total loyalty. Powell also had such a feel for Carter's thought processes that he became a philosophical alter ago of the candidate. Even though Powell had no prior experience in the job, these qualities made him credible and successful.

Good press secretaries often don't come from the world of journalism, although many have served, at some time or another, as reporters. One former U.S. senator admits that his first press secretary "was a guy in a VW van who got a flat tire as he was passing through my home town. He went to work for the local paper and was covering my campaign in its infancy. We got along well and he quit to be our campaign press secretary. By the time I left the senate, he was my administrative assistant and chief of staff."

And while some press secretaries might come from chance encounters, most come from having worked in other campaigns, local or state political parties, or public relations firms.

The search for a press secretary should include checking out the reputations and past experiences of all the potential candidates. There are many campaigns that have made the mistake of hiring a press secretary who seemed perfect, and allowing that individual to become integrally involved with the media—only to later discover that the individual is temperamental, devious, or inept. Imagine trying to break ties with a bad press secretary without that employee turning around and poisoning their media contacts against you.

THE IMPORTANCE
OF A
MEDIA CONSULTANT

Television didn't become a significant political weapon until the 1960s. But from the 1970s into the 1990s, it became not only the dominant means of political advertising, but in many cases, the one that no campaign except the smallest could afford to go without. Today most statewide, congressional, and other "large" campaigns are won in large part by the candidate who utilizes television most effectively. The growth of cable and digital television has widened the field so that even small campaigns, with limited resources, can often afford to utilize television as part of their strategy.

For campaigns that are low budget or, more importantly, have a smaller number of voters to reach, cable television can be utilized and its cost is surprisingly low. Most cable carriers have their own production companies who can cheaply produce a simple ad. Remember: in local or small district races, the most important element is name identification. Take the single most popular issue of the campaign and link it with the name of the candidate. Then make a cable buy that emphasizes repetition of the ad; flashing up "Elect Bill Jones—Protect Homeowner's Rights" one hundred times will be much more effective than running a thirty-second ad ten times. Today's viewer is a constant "channel surfer," so go for frequency.

When making cable buys, be sure you are targeting the channels that the people most likely to vote will be watching. This will vary from location to location, but statistics indicate that female voters wait a little longer to make their final choice, and they also turn out to vote in higher numbers. Any candidate would be wise, therefore, to consider programming aimed at such an important demographic segment of the electorate.

When candidates want to use larger television venues, such as broadcast stations, a campaign must turn to the talents of true political ad experts. Even at this highest level of specialization, talent levels, as well as fees, can vary greatly. But the most respected names in the business are not hard to find.

Dane Strother and his father Ray are among America's best-known political advertising gurus, particularly in the field of television. The elder Strother has been involved in some of the nation's top campaigns and has served as president of the National Association of Campaign Consultants. The younger Strother has taken his father's lead and has become a nationally recognized expert in the area of campaign media. Dane Strother is a frequent guest on virtually all of the national political talk shows.

☆

(The following excerpt is from a paper published by Dane Strother. He kindly allowed us to reprint it here.)

Television commercials are the B-52s of a political campaign. They can virtually carpet-bomb a community or state; the political landscape is inexorably altered in their wake. Television has also changed political campaigns. At one time the national parties were the central medium of elections; rallying the faithful on the first Tuesday in November was their main function. Today the Democratic and Republican Parties are basically relegated to the role of raising money to buy more and more television.

In general terms, a television spot is produced either to create a problem for an opponent or solve a problem for a client. Even seemingly innocuous spots are laying a base for a future attack or response. But every spot is different, and each campaign requires a unique approach. Consultants who try to use cookie-cutter ads and simply plug one candidate into another candidate's spots will eventually fail. Candidates should he wary if a consultant assures him or her that "this script always works." For whom, where, how?

Yet, much as people may deny it in conversation, television ads can work—they can make a hero look like a villain, stir voter anger, seize hearts, and capture minds. Most of all they provide information about candidates and campaigns to the majority of Americans who read and research little about who or what they vote for. In all, today, politics is television and television is politics—second only to a candidate in importance to a campaign.

Costs: Television, like any weapon of modern war, is tremendously expensive to create, deploy, and maintain. Most middle and down-ballot campaigns and even some congressional campaigns cannot afford the cost, or can only buy time sporadically. This is especially true in big markets like New York, Los Angeles and, to a lesser degree, Chicago, where it is unlikely that anything but a well-funded, statewide campaign can afford air time.

Another problem with the expenses of television is that its rates are volatile. Radio and television rates reflect the number of people who see or hear them; it is much less expensive to buy television in Des Moines than in New York. One buys television not by the number of spots but by the gross rating point (GRP). Arbitron, a rating service, determines how many people watch a certain show in a certain market. For example, we know that Seinfeld had a rating of 32, while no cable show enjoys a rating of even 1. A 32 means that 32 percent of viewers who are camped in front of a television while Seinfeld is airing are watching the show.

So buying an ad on Seinfeld would cost a great deal more than buying a show that had only, say, a 6 share. Television time purchase rates are set at a cost per point. A purchase of 100 points yields enough spots for everyone in a market to have seen a commercial once. One thousand points of television ensures that the average person sees a spot ten times. The cost per point is set for each of the 211 markets in America, and every market has a slightly different cost. For example, the cost per point in Baton Rouge, Louisiana, is roughly $32; in Atlanta, with ten times higher population, 0.3 point is roughly $300.

Buying television is a science. It is not enough to simply produce a spot and throw it on the air. The key is determining what shows a campaign's targets are watching, and ensuring the spots run during those shows. Saturday morning cartoons are out because children can't vote. But if the target audience for a campaign is working-class women over fifty who have little education, then soap operas are prime buys.

Regardless of when it runs, no ad stands alone. The office-seekers of October have to compete not just with AT&T, Coors, and the local Buick dealer, but also hundreds of other candidates for all sorts of other races. The explosion of advertising clutter means a spot must be hammered home over and over before the message is retained. Where a campaign might have once run a spot for 600 points, today 1,200 or 1,300 points are necessary. While we who make political ads try to distinguish ours from the pack, in the end it is understandable that voters might disconnect from so many similar messages, stagings, and plot lines. The result is increasing expenses to distribute less information with diminishing returns.

Accordingly, the goal for a political producer is to make a spot that has production values and a quality that stands up to the national ads that often *hookend it on television without costing a fortune. Political producers are exceedingly adroit at making television quickly and cheaply.*

A well-run campaign spends 75 percent of its war chest on television or mail. The idea is to keep overhead—salaries, candidate travel, and research costs—low so that the majority of resources are spent communicating with voters. In essence, a campaign is nothing more than a vehicle to deliver a message to voters; that message is a candidate's sales pitch. Giving voters a reason to support a candidacy is the only way to win a political campaign. And the more times a voter hears the message—assuming it is a message they want to hear and that it is delivered well—the more likely that voter is going to remember the message.

Included in the 75 percent earmarked for communication is the cost of production. A rough guide is that production costs 10 percent of the actual time hue. This varies according to the producer's ego and ability to keep costs down. Political advertising differs greatly from commercial products advertising in the directness and cost of the production. Political producers are always looking for a way to keep production costs to a minimum. It is unusual for one to cost more than $10,000, or about a tenth of what a consumer ad costs to make.

POSITIVE, CONTRASTIVE, AND NEGATIVE ADS

There are basically three different types of political television commercials: positive, contrastive, and negative. The mix and use of these three genres seems to change virtually every election cycle: no "lessons" are permanent.

All three ad types are essentially used to define both candidates. The idea is to paint beautiful pictures of one's client and a less than appealing view of the opponent. Polls are used to determine what aspect of a candidate's life or views might be attractive to the voters. For example, if the fact that a candidate is a self-made success moves undecided voters to him, then the television ad shows and tells that story: "John Doe is an up-by-the-bootstraps American success story. He's turned his life from challenge to fortune by believing he could, by working hard, being honest, and standing up when tough times would knock most people down."

Positive ads seldom if ever mention the opponent. Rather, they may offer an introduction to a candidate and his family, testimonials from people he has helped, or an explanation of what he hopes to do if elected. Each firm has a different philosophy, but in the 1998 election cycle we used more positive ads, packed with more information, than we once did because they are more compelling and because of the necessity of providing a lot of information in a short time.

Positive ads are the backbone of a good political campaign. But a good, positive ad begins setting up a contrast with the opponent without being obvious. In that sense, a positive ad can contain implied critiques of the opposition. This is because ultimately campaigns are about differences. Voters have to reach for one lever or another in the voting booth and they usually know little more than they have gleaned from television ads or from neighbors or friends who got their information from television ads. A campaign must give voters a reason to support a certain candidate while at the same time providing a reason not to support the opponent.

This said, the rules of negativity are changing. In 1998, for the first time, political professionals began to see that harsh negative ads were backfiring. For a decade the pundits and national press corps had bemoaned the fact that campaigns were little more than intellectual mud wrestling. Year after year, however, political professionals would use negative information about their opponent and see a positive effect: it seemed a textbook truism that "attacks work."

But a funny thing happened on the way to victory. Voters finally had enough of the malicious tactics. They seemed to be genuinely tiring of slashing, demeaning ads and reacted by tuning out the message and turning against the messenger. They are still receptive to information that is not complimentary to a candidate, but it must be delivered in a delicate manner: a scalpel rather than a chainsaw. For example, in one 1998 governor's race, the Republican candidate spent hundreds of thousands of dollars attacking his Democratic opponent, even before the opponent became the official nominee. The Republican tried to make sound objectionable dozens of votes that the Democrat had made in the state legislature. For four months he aired one negative ad after another. According to the old manual, this was good politics: define your opponent before he gets a chance to define himself.

For the most part the attacks were factual. The Democrat had made more than 50,000 votes and each for a good reason, but the attacks were out of context. To the voters' credit, they understood that. The Republican's tactless campaign was defeated by 10 percentage points; he vows he will never run again. He was done in by not noticing that the electorate was changing.

This example does not herald the end of negative ads by any means. But the question now is: What is a negative ad? Is it negative to point out that an opponent truly wants to abolish the national Department of Education? Or to explain that an opponent supports school vouchers, or does not?

Today's voter is much more responsive to what are called comparative ads. Eschewing screaming or name-calling, the best of the comparative ads simply put both candidates side by side and measure their records. Since today's wily voter refuses to believe an unsubstantiated charge, it is imperative to include documentation of every charge leveled. Indeed, 1998 focus group research taught professionals that using the banner of a newspaper headline in addition to the headline and article when substantiating a charge makes it more believable than just using the headline. The more information the better.

A candidate's gender has also largely become irrelevant. Both men and women must fully explain themselves, their platforms, and their charges. There was a time when spots for female candidates were softer or less aggressive, but those days are over, and voters see little difference between male and female candidates. Exceptions are "gender gap" ads. For example, the 1996 Mary Landrieu for U.S. Senate campaign presented a series of spots which featured only women exclusively on day-time television. The idea was to run a gender gap by speaking about a couple of topics that resonated with women more than men. Democrats must run gender gaps to win in the South and that sometimes requires specialized ads, but increasingly voters disdain pandering and want to know what the office-seeker will do for them.

THE RESEARCH IMPERATIVE

At one time, consultants created television with little more direction than a gut feeling or an idea from a friend or campaign employee. The lore of spots being written on the back of cocktail napkins is widespread. Single-malt whisky often served as a muse, and a campaign's strategy would change with the moon. Those days are gone.

If a modern consultant tells a candidate he or she has a "hunch," this is a signal to find a new consultant. Creating television commercials has become as much science as art. Tens of thousands of dollars are spent on research prior to the first draft of a script.

First there is an extensive interview of a candidate. Who is he or she? What makes them tick? What are they truly passionate about? Often this interview is taped on a home video camera and held for future reference. Then issues are discussed. Some candidates are willing to switch from unpopular positions, like opposing the death penalty. Others are resolute in their core beliefs and intransigent despite the risk of espousing an unpopular stance. Depending on the issue, the intransigence can cost a candidate a race. In a representative democracy, it is imperative that a candidate share the views of the voters.

Following the interview, a media consultant will travel with a candidate to see how he or she moves and interacts with people, and whether the campaign work is relished or endured. Speech patterns, intensity, delivery, and style are studied for days. The reason is simple: ultimately a consultant must capture a candidate's entire being on film. This is no easy task, as people rarely play themselves well on television.

The next step, then, is opposition research—conducted on the client as well as the opponent. Everyone is reluctant to expose skeletons and gaffes made over a lifetime; and even now so many office-seekers naively assume "it won't come out." Often clients promise there is nothing in their backgrounds that could be used against them in a campaign. Generally the research indicates they are wrong.

Once the opposition research is completed, a poll questionnaire is developed. This is often done with the help of all consultants in a campaign. It takes three to six days to conduct a poll and another week or so for a pollster to write a report. This accomplished, the campaign's message is determined and a media consultant begins thinking about the direction the campaign's communications should take. Candidates and consultants alike must recognize this truth: Polls should drive the content of television ads.

TELEVISION AND THE REAL WORLD

The above decisions cannot exist in a vacuum: real-life campaigning is often a series of compromises with reality, especially when dealing with the monetary drain of television. A case in point is the candidacy of Rose McKinney-James, an African-American woman coaxed into running for lieutenant governor in Nevada in 1998. She had never before run for office and the political climate was tough for a left-leaning Democrat in a Republican state. But McKinney-James possessed a charisma that can't be taught and she had the tools to become a very good candidate.

The great challenge for McKinney-James, however, was generating the necessary money and finding the motivation to make the enormous number of cold calls required to meet a financial goal. In raising money, candidates are competing against everyone on the ballot.

McKinney-James's opponent, Lorraine Hunt, was on the city council and managed to transfer some $400,000 from her city council re-elect account to her account for lieutenant governor. That put McKinney-James behind the curve. And with the lieutenant governor having little power in Nevada, it was difficult to convince contributors to give the maximum allowed contribution of $10,000.

Cash, or the lack of it, determined strategy. A poll indicated that education was the most important issue facing Nevada. School discipline was the specific focus. A decision was made to run McKinney-James as if she were aspiring to be the state's school principal. Rhetoric like, "We can't let two bad children hold hostage the education of 26 good kids," became part of the campaign's lexicon.

Ideally, the campaign would have run two positive ads spelling out how McKinney-James planned to put discipline back in the schools. The positives would have been followed by two negatives to turn voters away from Hunt. Then the campaign would close the final days with a wrap-up spot more positive than negative. That plan would have cost some $500,000; McKinney-James had only about $130,000.

In an attempt to overcome this financial deficit, the Democratic candidate's campaign employed a technique first created in 1992 in Arkansas called the "10-20." It is a means to run two spots for the price of one. The format calls for a 10-second negative ad delivered by an announcer. The spot fades to black for a second and a half and a positive ad follows. Crucially, voters believe they are two different ads, which is important because the candidate is then not held to blame for a negative ad. The problem with negative ads is that, although intended to drive up the unfavorable rating of one's opponent, they often slightly increase the unfavorable rating of the candidate running them as well.

In the Nevada race, the negative concerned Hunt voting to allow some restaurant owners to pay less than minimum wage. She was a restaurant owner herself, and the hope was that voters would find her position hypocritical. The positive portion of the ad featured McKinney-James speaking about putting discipline back into schools and holding students accountable. As she spoke she walked across an office set, and as the camera panned the governor moved into the shot to finish the spot by saying he strongly endorsed McKinney-James.

It was an attempt to run a negative, give a positive message, and offer an endorsement from the governor in 30 short seconds. Unfortunately, it violated the cardinal rule of trying to accomplish too many things in a 30-second spot. The lack of money for communications coupled with Hunt outspending McKinney-James by more than two to one made the outcome inevitable. The final vote was Hunt 50 percent, McKinney-James 40 percent, and lesser candidates carving up the remaining 10 percent.

The outcome was more of a reflection of money buying elections than a failed spot technique. Indeed the 10-20 format worked in what has become a famous case. In 1992, a 32-year-old woman named Blanche Lambert decided to move back to Arkansas from Washington and challenge her former boss in a Democratic primary. She had been a receptionist for Congressman Hill Alexander, who had served for 24 years. He did not take the challenge from the young woman seriously and by the time he recognized there was trouble it was too late.

Like McKinney-James, Lambert raised only enough money for one television commercial in the primary. The problem was that the district, Arkansas' 1st, required buying three media markets to properly communicate: Jonesboro, Little Rock, and Memphis.

Lambert used the 10-20 format. The negative was a seven-second clip showing Alexander denying he had bounced any checks at the now infamous, and closed, House Bank. As cartoon music played, a screen dropped over his face reading that Alexander bounced 114 checks. The following 20-second positive featured Blanche smiling and shaking hands with the words HONESTY, INTEGRITY, THE FUTURE, flashing across the screen. She won with 62 percent of the vote.

Lambert got married, served two terms, and retired due to complications from a pregnancy with twins. In 1998, she decided to run for the U.S. Senate seat vacated by Dale Bumpers. The primary had four major participants: Lambert-Lincoln; the sitting attorney general, who had also been the Democratic senate nominee two years prior; Winston Bryant Nate Coulter, a young, handsome man who had barely lost a race for lieutenant governor just two years prior; and a rich doctor who was running as the anti-politician.

Initial research indicated problems and opportunities. Focus groups told us that many older voters would not look favorably on a young woman with young children taking a full-time job as demanding as a U.S. Senate seat. The extrapolation was that a third of the electorate would simply not support Lambert-Lincoln because of this. But the focus groups also reported that the best way to overcome the concern was to show the candidate's husband, explain that he was a doctor, and that *the couple would raise their children together, as a team. The findings were incorporated into a poll and spots were written from the information.*

The research indicated that the best way to sell Lambert-Lincoln to the voters was to have her appear in person to speak to the camera. The budget of more than a million dollars for television allowed the campaign to run several different ads. Lambert-Lincoln, in most of the spots, looked directly into the camera and delivered 30-second pieces.

The ads worked: she ran first in the primary, won the runoff against Bryant, and defeated a far-right Republican by 60 to 40 percent. Lambert-Lincoln won not with "gut feelings" or genius, but by working hard and using research and polling to her advantage.

That is the reality of modern campaigning that unfortunately (and ironically) is little shown or publicized in mass media. The research, creative process, shooting, editing, and placement of television ads is a sober and clinical process—for good reason, because like war, people's lives and the country's welfare depend on it.

How to Find a Media Consultant

A list of experienced political media consultants can usually be obtained from a state's Republican or Democratic headquarters. Congressional candidates can turn to the House or Senate campaign committees of their political party in Washington. But most of the time candidates find their list of potential consultants by word of mouth. Talking to other elected officials (i.e., successful candidates!) usually helps generate a strong list of potential consultants.

After contacting the various consultants, the campaign should arrange to have its top leadership meet with each potential guru, and should view the reel of past commercials that he or she has produced.

During the interview process, these are some crucial questions that should be asked:

1. What is your win/loss record?

Any consultant who becomes defensive about this question should immediately be eliminated from contention.

2. Are you capable of providing general political strategy?

If the answer to this is "No, I just produce commercials," then, with the exception of a well-financed effort where a general consultant is also hired, this answer would also be a disqualifier. While a campaign's pollster often serves as chief strategist for the effort, it is rare for a media consultant not to also share in those duties. Remember, general political strategy now includes a critical Internet component. Any consultant worthy of your business should understand the importance of integrating the candidate's online presence and capabilities with the overall game plan for the campaign.

3. Are you capable of locating and working with local post-production facilities, assuming they are available?

This is crucial in smaller campaigns where it is usually more cost-effective to utilize local facilities, and in larger campaigns for quick turnaround of "response ads" (ads that require that you get a message or answer up on television on an expedited basis).

4. In larger budget campaigns the question should be asked: "Do you shoot actual footage (e.g., pictures of the candidate, his or her family, issue-oriented spots) on film or tape?"

If the answer is anything other than film, a candidate or campaign should forgo hiring that consultant if at all possible.

THE IMPORTANCE OF
POLLING AND A
POLLSTER

Political polling has become a mainstay of modern elections; indeed, it is unusual today for a campaign not to conduct one. But despite their frequency, polls are not well understood, even by many candidates. Before getting too far down the campaign trail, it is essential to understand what a poll is and what it is not. Properly used, it is an indispensable tool that can lead to victory. Alan Secrest, whose Washington, D.C., polling firm of Cooper & Secrest Associates has compiled a stellar record this decade in races across the country, puts it this way: "For all the mythology that surrounds political polling, its bottom-line function is that of an efficiency tool. Well-crafted polls should be used to help campaigns, at any level of elective office, to deploy limited resources—money, time, volunteers—most effectively in service to the goal of winning on election day."

In general, candidates usually conduct several polls over a period of time. The sequence begins with an early benchmark poll, designed to help the candidate formulate issues. Subsequent polls, known as trend and tracking polls, are used along the way to help supplement the original findings and to fine-tune the candidate's plan.

Glen Bolger, one of the nation's top Republican pollsters, explains the importance of the benchmark poll.

The goal of the benchmark survey is not to learn who is winning, but instead the goal is to figure out how to win the campaign. The benchmark survey is usually the first, and largest, survey done by the campaign. Sometimes, in a low-budget campaign, it is the only survey.

For all those reasons, it is crucial that the design of the questionnaire and the analysis be truthful and accurate. There are times I have done benchmark polls where the candidate has trailed by forty points, and yet I was dead certain we would win (and we did). There are other times where we've been ahead by five or six points, and yet I was certain we would lose (and we did!). A good poll is a planning tool, not a predictor.

The benchmark survey should serve as the primary driving force for the campaign plan. The questionnaire has to be well-designed. As a campaign team, you must be honest about what your opponent is going to say—and test their message, so you can make informed decisions about how to handle it. I like to test what I call "attack/defense" sequence—where we test what the opposition is going to say, and rebut it with our response. It helps sort out the terrain on which we would like to fight.

As a candidate, it is important that you provide your pollster with significant information prior to the design of the questionnaire—including both self and opposition research, potential themes, and key target groups. The self research is very important—as a candidate, you have to be honest with your team about problems from your past that you may think are no big deal, but could blow up the campaign if the team is not adequately prepared to handle them.

The benchmark should be used to lay out the strategy of the campaign. As a candidate, you have to be honest with yourself. There have been times when the potentially winning strategy from the poll is too much of a long shot to be realistic. In that case, you need to ensure that you are not wasting your family's time and money in a race that cannot be won (assuming winning is the goal). Make sure you are personally comfortable with what may be a losing investment before you make it.

The campaign's pollster works together with the other key people to help a campaign focus the rest of its resources more effectively. The poll should help you understand the impact of the political environment, identify key target groups, test themes, and focus the campaign's proactive and contrast messages.

While at various points, different elements of a given poll will be more important to a campaign than others, nearly every poll Cooper & Secrest Associates— one of the nation's top Democratic firms—conducts contains data in each of these categories: the mood of the electorate, the personalities, the trial heats, and the issues. Taken together, these findings yield a workable political battle plan. They help hone a theme, identify those issues that best communicate that theme, target key persuadable electoral subgroups, craft an evocative stump speech, and, especially in the tracking phase, determine the most effective mix and tone of paid communications (TV, radio, and mail), reset the candidate's schedule, and of course, bolster FUND-RAISING.

More and more, it is the rare campaign that flies blind without the benefit of the systematic insights polling can reveal about a given electorate. Essentially, polling throughout a campaign is analogous to using a road map to travel across the country. The poll should tell you how far it is from where you are at the outset to where you want to end up on election day. It should suggest the best, the most efficient route for getting to your political destination, as well as several alternate routes in the event of detours (i.e., the types of surprises that come up in almost every campaign).

To carry the analogy one step further, you first survey—the benchmark survey is like a comprehensive road atlas; its focus is broad and strategic. A follow-up trend survey is like an updated state map. Are you on course? Has a new road, a new political opportunity opened up recently? Finally, the brief tracking polls, now a staple in the closing weeks of today's campaigns, are designed to provide quick, tactical guidance at the end of the campaign, much like pulling into a service station near the end of your trip to find out now many blocks down or how many blocks over your destination is.

My point is that good polling accomplishes something for you. It is workable. A poll—an inquiry into the electorate's opinions—is insufficient if its focus is simply who is ahead or who is behind. Instead, it should be crafted to help the candidate find and implement every strategic and tactical advantage and potential advantage available to him or her during the campaign. What are your strengths and weaknesses, and what are your opponent's? What is there about this longtime incumbent that makes him vulnerable to a challenge? Is it his character, his performance, his record, his responsiveness—some combination of all of these? How well does his or her profile match what the city or county is looking for in its mayor, its county executive, or the state in its governor? Which elements of his or her background should he or she emphasize, and which should be de-emphasized?

These are the kinds of questions a good poll can answer and should answer. Naturally, the better the research that goes into the preparation for the poll—including a rigorous examination of the incumbent's record, his votes, statements he has made that may be contradictory, and so forth, as well as the challenger's background on applicable dimensions—the better the poll.

In the end, a typical poll provides information in four areas: (1) the landscape or backdrop for the campaign (partisan preference, ideology, relative levels of optimism, what factors voters are using to make a decision, an initial look at a candidate's job performance); (2) personalities (personal appeal, name recognition, an open-ended look at the candidates, comparisons on certain traits and characteristics); (3) the trail heats (an identification of each candidate's core support and core opposition, as well as a close look at soft or movable voters) ; and (4) issues (what are the issue priorities, which segments of the electorate feel *most strongly about which issues, and how do the respective issue positions of these candidates impact their election strategies).*

Of course a poll is flawed and often damaging if it is allowed to be biased by a flawed questionnaire or sample design, inadequate interviewing, or faulty data analysis.

How a Poll Is Conducted

Pollster Alan Secrest has a simple set of guidelines for conducting a political poll. Given his enviable track record, it would be wise to keep his list in mind when evaluating potential pollsters, to determine if they are familiar with these basic rules of the game.

☆ ☆ ☆ ☆ ☆

1. Stop—Look—Listen

The first step in putting together an effective poll is to listen—to be willing to set aside the conventional wisdom and put the campaign's collective ear to the ground to see if there aren't rumblings of change in your district's political topography. The campaign must insist on being instructed by what has gone before, but not slavishly devoted to it.

2. Sample Design

Here we are concerned with deciding whom to interview for the poll and finding the best means for reaching them. Naturally it is critical to avoid the introduction of bias throughout the polling process—in questionnaire design, in interviewing, in processing data, and in analyzing it. If the sample is constructed in a flawed fashion that permits bias to influence the outcome, the poll is virtually worthless from the outset.

It is important to remember that the goal of sampling is to give every likely voter in a particular election an equal chance to be selected for interviewing. Literally speaking, this is not always possible within a practical time frame and budget, since, for example, some people don't have telephones. Nevertheless, "equal chance" should be the guiding principle of sample design. Part of the design process should also include a series of screening questions at the outset of the questionnaire designed to winnow the sample to eliminate unlikely voters.

A threshold question for a poll is how many interviews should be conducted to achieve an accurate result? Alan Secrest usually recommends the following minimum numbers: local and legislative races—four hundred; congressional—five hundred; major statewide races—eight hundred. Regardless of the size of the sample, the goal is to find the best balance between overall sample error and the need for accurate subgroup analysis, including gender, age, geography, race, and so forth.

The matter of whom to call is usually resolved by using listed numbers in a telephone directory, random digit dialing, cross-reference directory with street listings, or registered voter lists. Which method to use in what circumstance is a matter of debate among pollsters and often boils down to what has worked for the pollster in the past.

3. Questionnaire Design

The questionnaire, the document containing the questions to be asked in the polling interviews, should be designed in a collaborative effort between the candidate and the principals in the campaign, and then refined by the pollster. Most candidates worth their salt have some idea of what the issues are. First-time candidates who have no public record can test the reaction to their professional or civic records, or to issues they have championed as private citizens. Incumbents or prior office holders must test reaction to their public record as well as to mistakes they have made. One thing is certain: the better the input, the better the output. Or put another way, the quality of the poll depends on the quality of the information on which it is based.

4. Data Collection

It is imperative that the telephone interviews be conducted by a team of carefully trained, carefully supervised professionals. Most nationally known pollsters do this in-house. Cooper & Secrest Associates performs this task with a one-hundred-line phone bank with careful electronic monitoring. Often this work is keyed directly into a computer for rapid analysis.

5. Data Processing

In processing the data generated by the interviews, Cooper & Secrest uses a custom-designed software package to process the raw data in terms of aggregate response, and subgroup by subgroup responses. The subgroups include region, race, gender, and party. One of the key elements here is to be sure that the raw, aggregate totals conform to the demographics of the sample and conform to the known or presumed electoral characteristics. For example, in a state with an African-American population of 30 percent, it would be inaccurate to have a sample with only 20 percent African-American responses.

When necessary, statistical weights are applied to the data to bring the sample into line. This process must be done with the utmost care. The data for the subgroups is then put into tables called crosstabs. A proper analysis of the crosstabs by a competent professional pollster can unlock winning issues. They can tell the candidate, for example, what white women over fifty think of an issue as opposed to white women from eighteen to thirty. Differences between the opinions of urban blacks and rural blacks can be deciphered. The analysis of the subtleties of the data is one of the most important functions of the pollster. It is easier to take a poll than to analyze it correctly.

6. Presentation

The candidate and the pollster should meet in person with the campaign staff for a formal presentation of the findings. No candidate ever has time to pore over the details of the poll. In a presentation, important focus is given to the issues raised by the data and questions can be answered. The presentation of the poll is time well spent. A poll is an investment which, used properly, will return handsome dividends. It should save you money in targeting your resources. It should also help the candidate raise money when properly presented to potential contributors. The poll is also most useful in preventing overreaction or underreaction to campaign events either expected or unexpected.

A poll is not a magic wand. It is not a substitute for good judgment or responsiveness. But it is a nearly indispensable means of maintaining a continuing dialogue with the voters and, in the process, substantially increasing the chances for victory.

HOW TO FIND A POLLSTER

Virtually anyone can call themselves a pollster. The best way to find one, as we have suggested for so many other campaign positions, is to ask other successful candidates who they have used in prior races.

But beware: Some so-called pollsters will use bait-and-switch tactics in order to try and get a campaign's business. For example, they will suggest that they can produce a poll that shows the candidate doing much better than the candidate suspects. They accomplish this by using the "push-polling" techniques that we discuss elsewhere in the book. Indeed, almost every candidate allows "push" questions to obscure their view or create a rose-colored future. Here's a great example from our statewide contest.

MATT: As I reached the last months of my battle against Pierre, it was painfully obvious that I had nowhere near the name identification, or base number of Republican voters, to win the race. My own October poll showed me with only 19 percent of the committed vote, compared to Pierre's 53 percent. So, of course, we started "push polling," asking how people felt about various votes Pierre had taken on controversial issues. Lo and behold, when we asked them to reconsider their vote, the numbers flip-flopped and I was actually leading with 41 percent to Pierre's 28 percent.

There was only one problem—our campaign couldn't deliver the message on those votes. We were wasting valuable time in a fantasy world. And valuable money that could have been better spent buying general positive ads that would have increased my name identification. The race naturally narrowed, as all do, but the "push ballot" fantasy never came close to coming true—and Pierre ended up with well over 50 percent of the total vote!

THE IMPORTANCE
OF A
DIRECT MAIL EXPERT

George magazine, when listing its one hundred greatest moments of the century, placed Texan Richard Viguerie's invention of political direct mail at number sixty-two, between the McCarthy hearings and the desegregation of the military. Viguerie suggests that, while there is no simple rule, "I believe that the lower down on the ballot the office is listed, the greater the role for direct mail. For example, TV should play only a minor role, or no role at all in most state legislative races." He points out that "one of the greatest sins committed in a political direct mail is to overlook the fact that the people on your mailing list have certain characteristics that may vary. For example, the farmers in north Florida have different problems than young people in Fort Lauderdale. And those who are retired in Fort Lauderdale have different problems than young people who live in that same area, but who have children in school and are buying their first house. . . . A good direct mail consultant can get this information early in a campaign."

In recent years there has been a tendency among many top political experts to discount the value of direct mail. And certainly as a fund-raising tool it has seen better days. Those first "personalized" letters from big-name political leaders back in the 1970s and early '80s made voters feel special, and often resulted in significant financial donations by mail. But most Americans who are worthy of being on any "hit list" for direct mail fund-raising have been hit so many times that the gimmick is now viewed as what it is: a gimmick. In general these days, direct mail—when soliciting funds—at best simply recovers the cost of printing and mailing.

Direct mail, however, remains invaluable as a method of cost-effectively delivering a message.

We asked Ross Bates, one of the top Democratic direct mail experts in America, to explain the value of direct mail in the campaigns of the new millennium. His firm is one of the leading companies to provide assistance to Democratic governors, congressmen, and legislative caucuses.

☆

In an age dominated by television, many political observers believe that direct mail is an obsolete medium for persuasion. Nothing could be further from the truth. In fact, direct mail can target voters in ways that television cannot. Contrary to what some media consultants would have you believe, television is a broad-based medium that is only effective in sending out a general message to a widely diverse audience. Television advertisers can't expect their advertisements to be seen ONLY in the homes of African Americans, senior citizens, farmers, etc. In fact, there's no guarantee that they'll even be home, and if they are, there's no guarantee that they'll be tuned into the correct channel, when the advertisement airs. But you can almost always count on people checking their mail. And that's something that can make or break a political campaign.

In one of the first midwestern congressional campaigns to use direct mail, the losing candidate didn't understand its importance until it was too late. On election day, he had this to say: "I don't understand. About three weeks out, our poll numbers started to go down. There was nothing happening nationally. There was nothing happening locally. But, we started losing support and our opponent kept gaining." What happened was simple. The winning candidate began sending out persuasion mail three weeks prior to election day. The mail's effectiveness clearly took the losing candidate by surprise.

Simply using direct mail, however, isn't enough. It must be well thought out. Like all campaign messages, if the direct mail is good, it will connect with the needs and concerns of the voters. Great mail uses the best qualities of the print medium (graphics, effective copy, etc.), along with the technical skills necessary for specific message targeting. In other words, a great mail program aims the most persuasive messages at the most persuadable voters. By using polling data, along with the candidate's qualifications and background, a mail program can be created that is both compelling and credible.

There are several examples from the 1998 elections that illustrate this point. All the mailers mentioned were used for Democratic candidates in North Carolina legislative races; all dealt with the issue of education, but the approach was different for each mailing, depending on the political dynamics of the campaign. Positive mailers emphasize the assets and achievements of the candidate. For State Representative Richard Moore, we used Moore's background as a teacher and church group leader to connect him with the values of the district—a very important thing to do for a first-term incumbent in a conservative district. In creating the mailer for Senator Howard Lee, however, we used a specific legislative accomplishment to connect with voters interested in education by showcasing a record of achievement.

The same principle applies to a negative mailer. We use a key issue where the opponent is clearly on the wrong side to illustrate how he/she does not connect with the needs and concerns of the voters. This was the case with the negative mailer on education that we produced for the campaign against Bobby Ray Hall—again in a North Carolina legislative campaign. We showed a problem and how the incumbent Republican failed to solve the problem.

If done well, negative mail will be a help, not a hindrance. In fact, negative mail only backfires when it is off-line from the voters' concerns or if it is not believable. Sometimes, the most creative-looking negative mail fails to work because it is not relevant to the voters or it is so "over-the-top" that it is rendered unbelievable. What is or is not considered believable is often a matter of context. In the 1994 congressional elections, anything negative said about a candidate regarding his/her connection with President Clinton was considered believable by the voters, because of the 1994 political environment. Yet four years later, the negatives against President Clinton, while seemingly more serious, had little effect on the voters in congressional elections and often backfired on the Republicans.

So, what circumstances govern mail's effectiveness? Mail can deliver messages that can't go on television. Television is a broadcast medium. A 70-year-old man and a 38-year-old woman watching the seven o'clock news see the same commercial. So the content must be tailored to appeal to different segments of the electorate.

Mail, on the other hand, is a narrow-cast medium. It can be targeted so a particular piece will only be received by senior citizens, by women, or by voters in a certain part of the district. The message of the mailer can be much sharper and infinitely more connective with the specific concerns of the specific voter.

Sometimes an issue is of burning importance to a certain segment of the electorate and totally irrelevant, at best, to the rest of the district. This is yet another example of when mail can be very effective. For example, in a 1990 congressional race, we were given the assignment of increasing the incumbent's totals in a traditionally Republican county in the suburbs. We concentrated on local issues that would have been a waste of time and money had we tried to communicate them to the rest of the district.

Mail can support the campaign theme. Mail is often targeted to key swing voters in a state or district in order to reinforce the main campaign message being delivered by the dominant television media. Using polling and other data to target the swing voters, mail delivers a message, usually late in the campaign, that covers the same territory as the television media.

This is a technique most often used in statewide campaigns. In 1996, for example, we were called into the campaign of Jeanne Shaheen, who was running to be the first Democratic woman elected governor of New Hampshire. Polling indicated that younger women in the southern part of the state were the most important swing voters. These voters were especially responsive to a contrastive message showing Shaheen's opponent's extreme positions. We produced three mailings along this theme for the last two weeks of the campaign, helping Shaheen win the election.

Mail can be the most cost-effective way to deliver the main message. In many instances, mail is the predominant medium used to communicate the main campaign message. In large and expensive media markets, mail is a more cost-effective means of reaching the voters than television or radio. This is especially true in the Los Angeles and San Francisco media markets, where modern direct mail first developed, because the price for using television and radio was, and still is, very expensive.

In 1992 in Georgia, Don Johnson challenged incumbent Ben Jones in the 10th Congressional District. About 65 percent of the district was in the expensive Atlanta media market. The rest was in the more affordable Augusta market. The campaign decided to use mail exclusively to deliver the message in the Atlanta market and used television exclusively in Augusta—thereby maximizing the campaign's resources in both markets. (Good political mail is most likely when all consultants in a campaign are working as a team, more concerned with winning the election than with turf wars over who will be spending more of the campaign budget. Good media consultants like Saul Shorr, who worked on the Don Johnson campaign, understand this.)

Mail works very well in a primary. Using mail as the major communication device is especially useful in primary elections. In a 1992 New York election, we helped Nydia Velazquez become the first Puerto Rican woman elected to Congress. She defeated an incumbent, Stephen Solarz, who went on New York *television and spent $2.5 million, ten times more than Velazquez. Yet Velazquez's targeted mail, to an ethnically and geographically diverse district, helped her win a huge upset.*

Needless to say, mail works and works well. Still, there will always be those who subscribe to the philosophy that television is the only viable medium for campaign advertising. The truth of the matter is, television does work. But, a smart campaign knows that it isn't wise to put all of your apples into one barrel. A good campaign uses all forms of media, together and cooperatively, to get its message out to the voters. Nothing's foolproof when it comes to politics, but a solid media mix, using mail, can—and oftentimes does—produce winning results.

How to Find a Direct Mail Expert

Sophisticated political consultants have access to numerous potential direct mail experts. Generally, the creation of direct mail pieces, their printing and mailing will all be the responsibility of one professional or company.

However, many local or smaller campaigns don't have access to these "pros" (and many large campaigns get ripped off because they fall prey to the concept that "political consultants" have better "political lists"). And what if the campaign is a low-budget effort and cannot afford a professional, big-name direct mailer? The answer may well be found in a hunt of direct mail houses, or inquiry into local magazines or charitable organizations, where a volunteer who is familiar with the process might be found.

A local marketing, advertising, or printing firm can easily help find an up-to-date mailing list. Even better, most county, municipal, and state governments make the voter lists available on tape, CD, or in other forms that can easily be sorted by region, district, or zip code.

The key to good direct mail is to target, target, target. That's why someone with a detailed list of actual recent voters, broken down by party, gender, and frequency of voting, is of immense value to a campaign.

Consider the case of one female candidate for a state legislative post. Having vaulted past three of four male contenders, she found herself face-to-face with a longtime veteran of that state's legislature. Her college intern researcher had found an off-the-cuff remark that the incumbent male had made about the importance of a secretary "having large breasts." And although the female candidate might have been a neophyte, her direct mail expert was far more experienced. In a matter of days, a direct mail piece quoting the "male pig" with his big breast observation was out the door to female voters who had voted in her party's primary in the past two elections—hard-core voters most likely to be offended by the careless and cruel comment. She won the runoff and served for almost a decade before retiring from the state senate.

In searching for a direct mail consultant, the criteria, in descending order of importance, should be:

1) **Does the direct mail source have lists of actual voters?**

2) **Can the lists be broken down into segments such as district, gender, party, age, ethnicity?**

3) **Have the names been updated within the past three to six months for accurate address, phone, etc.?**

4) **Can the lists help a candidate determine the most likely voters?**

This is crucial in campaigns where finances are thin. If there are only twenty thousand households that can be mailed to, they darn well better be likely to vote.

THE IMPORTANCE OF
A SPEECHWRITER

A good speechwriter is valuable—and rare. They're rare not because speech-writing is an esoteric discipline, but because in order for them to be effective, the candidate must work with them. It's a partnership. Unfortunately, it's too often a limited partnership.

Speechwriters don't have to be dazzling wordsmiths. In fact sometimes it's better if they aren't. A haughty writer can get so caught up in writing pretty that he or she forgets that they are writing for you, not for their own literary legacy.

Certainly basic literacy—including cultural literacy—is essential in a speechwriter. More important, however, is to get someone with whom you share common views and mutual trust. Especially trust. If you're guarded around your speechwriter, he or she is never going to reflect your thoughts or present your views accurately. If your speech-writer is afraid to criticize you, to tell you something stinks, they will be severely handicapping your campaign.

To keep your speechwriter informed, make him or her part of your campaign's inner circle. If speechwriters could read minds, they'd be answering calls for the psychic hot line. Keep them involved with all aspects of the campaign. Have them travel with you and work with your staff.

If you keep your speechwriter out of the loop and in some lonely cloister, he's going to lose touch. When he does, he's going to compensate by overwriting. You'll find yourself with speeches that look great on paper, but read poorly in front of a crowd. In fact, you are likely to find that the phrases the speechwriter is most pleased with are the first ones you need to cut. That's because natural speech doesn't sound like poetry—it has its own flow. Make sure your speechwriter writes that way.

Another reason it's important to trust—and preferably to like— your speechwriter is so that you can open yourself up. Tell the speechwriter about your past, the places you've been, your hobbies, and your family life. Somewhere in these true confessions will be something that illuminates your entire makeup, something that inspired you to become a potential public servant. A good speechwriter can use this kind of material to spotlight who you are.

Don't edit these memories for political appropriateness. That's the speechwriter's job. You can always delete anything embarrassing before you actually speak. For now, just chat in idle moments. Long car rides are ideal. Let them read your writing, listen to your conversations, even taping them if needed. If they work at it, they will get better and better at capturing your speech rhythms.

Speechwriters should also stay informed about popular culture in general. Like you, they should read the newspaper: the headlines, yes— but the sports and the advice columns and the funnies, too. Connecting policy issues to everyday life is a way to make the speaker's views more appealing to voters.

Don't expect miracles from your speechwriter (unless you're paying a miraculous fee). A speechwriter's job is to polish the glass so that voters can see what's inside the candidate. If what's inside amounts to very little, mere words will be inadequate cover.

There are three speechwriters in the modern era who have distinguished themselves beyond all others. Theodore "Ted" Sorensen was John Kennedy's ultimate ghost writer. Kennedy, a gifted writer in his own right, crafted wonderful lines, but it was Sorensen who gave Kennedy's speeches (as well as his Pulitzer Prize–winning book *Profiles in Courage*) their crisp, natural flow. Sorensen's great gift was his ability to collaborate and to supply the continuity of thought and phrase to Kennedy's ideas so that everything he said made sense, and seemed to build to a logical conclusion.

Another memorable speechwriter trained in the world of college debate was a brilliant wordsmith named Bob Shrum. Shrum pushed Ted Kennedy to, in turn, push Jimmy Carter for a debate in their 1980 primary fight. Shrum knew that, along with the help of debate guru James Unger and Harvard Law's preeminent star Laurence "Larry" Tribe, he could provide Kennedy with speeches that would leave Carter in the dust.

But Shrum's plan was not to be; Carter wouldn't take the bait. Having personally dealt with Shrum, Unger, et al., there's little doubt in our minds that Carter would have found such a debate a potentially deadly scene. But having also known Hamilton Jordan, Jody Powell, and company, we aren't surprised that the Carter team never fell for the ploy.

And so Shrum's shining moment came, instead, in turning Ted Kennedy, the Democratic party's runner-up for the nomination, into its 1980 convention winner. Kennedy's concession speech ended with one of the great conclusions of modern politics:

"For me, a few hours ago, this campaign came to an end. For all those whose cares have been our concern, the work goes on, the cause endures, the hope still lives, and the dream shall never die." It was classic Shrum. Shrum's most powerful weapon was that of cadence, his ability to create a rhythm of peaks and valleys. Kennedy latched onto Shrum's style and moved the 1980 convention hall from melancholy wandering to glorious exuberance.

The third great speechwriter of the modern political era was Peggy Noonan, a woman who had all the personal dramatic flair of a Hollywood star. And it was her own sense of presence and style that brought out the heart and emotion of Ronald Reagan in words and phrases that were often beyond him.

After the traumatic explosion of the space shuttle Challenger in 1986, it was Noonan's guiding hand that wordsmithed Reagan's unforgettable tribute to the shuttle's crew. Reagan's delivery was his own, but it was Noonan's brilliant paraphrase of a beloved poem that so memorably described the shuttle's crew slipping "the surly bonds of earth" to "touch the face of God." The goose bumps and tears these words produced were indicative of the talented Noonan touch.

Speechwriters can also cause great embarrassment. Consider the legislator who hired a speechwriter to prepare him for the speech of his life. When the time came, the legislator began delivering the high-sounding phrases in a booming voice. He came to the end of one phrase with a flourish and then delivered with fervor this line inserted by his speechwriter: "Ladies and Gentleman, stop . . . tell a joke." Only when the audience began to laugh did he realize that he was to have told his favorite joke at that point in the speech. It was too late, and he himself became the joke.

THE SCHEDULER AND OTHER IMPORTANT CAMPAIGN STAFF

No job (other than the press secretary) has as much hands-on interaction with the public as that of the scheduler. Be it a paid or volunteer position, even the smallest of campaigns must have one—and only one—person who ultimately makes the decision about which events and appointments the candidate will attend. The most sophisticated of political offices (e.g., the president, U.S. Speaker of the House, etc.) have full scheduling departments. But even with scores of individuals assigned to this important area, there is always one chief scheduler. After all, many invitations are declined and someone has to be the bad guy—and it surely can't be the candidate.

The chief scheduler must be a highly organized individual who is accessible, friendly, and capable of handling intense stress with grace and at least an outward veneer of pleasantness.

Scheduling conflicts will inevitably arise. They should be resolved based upon what will do the most good for the campaign. The candidate should make the final determination, but the blame must always go to the scheduler. The scheduler must be prepared to fall on the sword, to take the blame for the inexplicable "conflict" that keeps a candidate from appearing at a given event—and he or she must also be willing to "try and reschedule" these events most apologetically.

Another indispensable campaign position is that of a good CPA, or at the very least a bookkeeper, to stay on top of the myriad financial disclosures that modern campaigns require. Do not take the recording of donations and the reporting of all necessary information lightly. Have someone who thoroughly knows the legal requirements for your campaign (preferably a lawyer) also look over everything from financial reporting to local campaign sign ordinances. We cannot stress this point enough, and we both have experienced the misery of having either relied on bad advice or simply overlooked required filings or disclosures. Virtually every elected official and candidate, at some point in time, has too. The goal is to always remain honest and ethical, and to try your very best to minimize such mistakes.

MATT: Whenever problems do arise, move immediately to find the very best professionals to provide both advice and assistance. For example, I was chairing the Newt Gingrich 1992 reelection effort when the now-infamous "Congressional Check-Bouncing Scandal" arose. Apparently, scores of congressmen were writing personal checks out of the House of Representatives' bank account without sufficient funds to cover them. Gingrich, who was at that time House Minority Whip, was one of those who had allegedly bounced checks. Rather than argue with the media, I hired a reputable accounting firm to create a full chronological ledger of all of Gingrich's checks. The accounting firm was able to prove that Gingrich had almost always deposited his checks, but that the House Bank was waiting several days before crediting the deposits. Letting professionals do their job made it possible to prove that not only Gingrich, but many other congressmen, both Democrat and Republican, were not knowingly going around writing bad check after bad check.

And professional assistance is not the only additional talent needed. While no one may like being referred to as "the driver," every political candidate needs one. The person who drives the candidate to events, particularly in campaigns that are small and cannot enjoy the luxury of having advance teams or other on-site assistance available, must be articulate and bright. Many times this driver will be viewed by the public as an important link to the candidate. He or she must be capable of dealing with questions, working out logistical problems, even serving as a makeshift spokesperson. Many of the really great political consultants and managers (as well as many great candidates) began their careers in their early twenties by serving in this multifaceted, if occasionally demeaning, position. It is also true that the driver spends more time with the candidate than anyone else in the campaign, and a bond develops between them akin to the bonds forged in a foxhole in the fields of battle. Many drivers become influential advisors in the administrations of successful candidates. Remember Jody Powell?

VOLUNTEERS

Every political campaign must deal with a nagging question: What to do with the volunteers? Ah, the volunteers—those true believers, brimming with enthusiasm and energy and waiting to be told what to do. The problem with volunteers is that not only do they usually not have a clue about what it takes to win a race, if they are ignored they can quickly turn into the campaign's worst critics. A frequent refrain of the disgruntled volunteer is that "I called and offered to help, and I never heard a word. They must not want my help." This is normally said to the candidate's wife's best friend in the hope that it will get back to the candidate. With friends like that, who needs enemies? On the brighter side, if the campaign has a plan in place for the proper utilization of volunteers, they can create life and excitement in a campaign that will bolster the candidate's spirits.

A classic example of the effective use of volunteers was the presidential campaign of peanut farmer Jimmy Carter in 1976. Governor

Carter had created quite a stir with his gubernatorial inauguration speech in 1971 when he declared that "the time for discrimination in Georgia is over." He made the cover of *Time* magazine, and was a "New South" governor whose support was prized. In 1972, therefore, he got to size up the current crop of Democratic presidential candidates as they trooped dutifully through the state to meet him and try to gain his support.

This parade of candidates included the ebullient Senator Hubert Humphrey, on whom Amy spilled chocolate cake (to his good-natured surprise), as well as Senator Ed Muskie, who asked Carter at breakfast, "What is the name of this amusement park we're going to be subjected to today?" (Carter privately would have disdained such an attitude since he relished the chance to press the flesh, a talent he had elevated to an art form.) Then came the solid but tired-looking Senator "Scoop" Jackson and the eventual nominee, Senator George McGovern. What the candidates didn't know was that Carter was coming to understand, as he met them for the first time, that in most cases he had more to offer than they did. When he began to tell his staff and close friends of his intentions, most were supportive but skeptical. We remember the retort of his wonderful mother, Miss Lillian, when Carter told her that he was going to run for president. "President of what?" she asked. He had campaigned for four long years to win the governorship. His belief was that if he could shake every hand in Georgia twice, he would win. As a result of this heroic grassroots effort, he had friends in every corner. Whatever obstacles Carter faced in a run for president, he had an army of true believers in Georgia who would walk through walls of fire for him. All of them wanted to help the campaign, but how?

The answer was the aptly named "Peanut Brigade." The nucleus was a group of close friends from his hometown of Plains. The idea was simple: Carter supporters would form small groups—from ten to thirty or more—and travel at their own expense to primary states with the sole objective of meeting voters and winning friends for Jimmy Carter. The Peanut Brigade was democratic; everyone worked together: bank presidents and silk-stocking lawyers knocked on doors alongside labor leaders and students. They attended meetings and handed out literature. They manned phones and stood on street corners with signs. Lodging was often provided by local Carter supporters in order to keep down expenses.

The campaign staff in each primary state directed the Peanut Brigade to whatever task was at hand. New Hampshire voters, jaded by too many campaigns, were astounded by these hordes of Georgians who had traveled so far to slog through the snow for their man. Maybe he was worth a second look! When Carter won the New Hampshire primary, he thanked the Peanut Brigade publicly. Suddenly, everyone wanted to join. People who had never even thought about getting involved in a campaign found themselves in faraway places asking strangers to vote for Jimmy Carter. Radio and television reporters began to seek out members of the Brigade for human-interest stories. There were stories about the youngest and the oldest, the famous and the obscure. Now legislators were getting into the act, along with state officials. Speeches were delivered on street corners, and television interviews were granted.

As the ranks swelled, opposing candidates began to notice. One volunteer was handing out brochures at the Brown County Raceway near Aberdeen, South Dakota, when Mo Udall walked up to shake hands. When he heard the southern accent, he exclaimed, "My God, the Peanut Brigade has invaded South Dakota!" Carter won the South Dakota primary to the surprise of everyone except himself, his family, and the Peanut Brigade.

The genius of the Peanut Brigade was that it cost the campaign very little money while still generating excitement, publicity, and votes. It also gave the campaign a grassroots feel that fit well with the image of the candidate. An unanticipated advantage was the psychological boost Carter got from seeing his Georgia friends in distant places. It was not unusual for a group of volunteers to show up late at night at some obscure airport and wait in the cold to greet his arrival. Carter would invariably stop to thank each of them personally, which spurred them on to even more sacrificial efforts. These efforts continued through the general election, and after Carter became president, he faithfully entertained Peanut Brigaders at the White House in appreciation for all they had done.

While most volunteer efforts cannot match those of the Peanut Brigade, there are many ways to harness volunteer energy. One statewide campaign had a postcard printed showing the candidate with his family on the front and a generic message of support for "my friend" on the back. Volunteers were asked to address anywhere from 10 to 250 of these cards to their personal friends, sign them, and return them to the campaign with postage for a mass mailing just before the election. Almost fifty thousand postcards went out to voters. For weeks after the election, the candidate would meet people who cited the postcard as the reason for their vote. This tactic works best in down-ticket or local races where most voters don't know the candidates and will take the word of a friend in the absence of other information from advertising. It is important that the cards be turned in to the campaign for mailing (with or without postage) to assure that they have actually been addressed.

Candidates soon learn that not all volunteers will follow through and complete assigned tasks, even though they may have the best of intentions. Then, too, there are times when all volunteers don't have good intentions. One rueful candidate tells the story of traveling to a rural county in the Deep South and engaging a volunteer to distribute literature in the precinct on election day. When the votes came in, the candidate got creamed in that county. Later, the candidate asked the state senator from the area what happened. "It's simple," said the senator. "I was for your opponent. I waited until you left town, and I went over to the volunteer's house and he gave me your literature, which I promptly threw in the trash. That 'volunteer' of yours was on my staff. We just wanted you to give us your literature."

Each campaign should devise a plan that will keep volunteers happy and helpful, if only marginally. One candidate asked persistent volunteers to look up telephone numbers for all the voters in a large metro county. The telephone numbers were never used, but the volunteers felt useful. Some campaigns have successfully trained volunteers to make telephone calls on behalf of the candidate, but experience teaches that if there is a vital campaign function to be performed, it is almost always more effective to hire trained professionals. A rude or uninformed telephone solicitor can do more harm than good.

The reality of modern-day campaigning is that the best thing a supporter can do for a candidate is to write a check and ask others to do the same. We all remember the nostalgic stories of John F. Kennedy's first campaign for Congress in Boston, when his mother and sisters organized coffees all over town where the young war hero could appear and work his charm. Today in a congressional or statewide race, there is little time for such activities unless the candidate has enough money to fund the campaign on his or her own. Otherwise, candidates must accept the fact that they cannot afford to participate in anything that does not generate money and/or planned publicity for the campaign.

Here is a checklist of "meaningful duties" that volunteers can help carry out:

Precinct work

* Preparing voter index cards
* Recruiting party workers and lists
* Calling people to get them to register to vote
* Poll clerk or registration clerk
* Poll watcher or registration watcher
* House-to-house canvassing
* Providing transportation to polls on election day
* Block captain or precinct captain

Campaign work

* Publicity
* Distributing literature
* Public speaking
* Planning and putting out mailings
* Arranging speaking engagements
* Manning sound trucks
* Speech-writing
* Preparing posters, streamers
* Research
* Putting up posters
* Filing
* Designing buttons, stickers, literature
* Calling people to get them to register to vote

- ★ Typing
- ★ Writing letters to the editor
- ★ Buying time and space in advertising
- ★ Web site design and construction
- ★ Web site maintenance
- ★ Meetings, rallies, social events
- ★ Planning programs
- ★ Ticket selling
- ★ Planning and running money-raising events
- ★ Decorations and arrangements
- ★ Acting as meeting master of ceremonies
- ★ Organizing parades
- ★ Bookkeeping (receipts and expenditures)
- ★ Obtaining speakers
- ★ Briefing speakers
- ★ Escorting speakers to meeting places
- ★ Planning and running rallies

In the end, it is the merger of product development and the talent to market that product that will determine whether a candidate's effort in this "mean world" of political business will succeed. So do yourself a favor, and arm your campaign with the best political minds you can find (and afford). We cannot guarantee you victory, but we can guarantee you an organized campaign that possesses the necessary elements to have a solid chance to win.

INTEGRATING THE INTERNET

Ten years ago, the Internet was simply a nonfactor in the world of political campaigns. No one, including us, had any idea that the next decade would see this powerful interactive electronic tool bring about an explosive communications revolution that would touch every aspect of our lives, including the business of politics. Now news about the Internet-specific fund-raising and communications prowess of the year 2000 presidential candidates dominates one out of every three headlines, and the World Wide Web has become a factor in even the smallest local political races. And all of this is with the political use of the Internet essentially in its infancy!

This chapter is dedicated to outlining for you the key players necessary for you to efficiently execute your campaign Internet plan, and the tools with which they need to be proficient. We want to wrap it up by talking about how to integrate this new and comprehensive tool into your overall strategy. While the Internet alone won't propel you into public office, efficient use of its potential can strengthen almost every aspect of your campaign. Conversely, refusing to recognize that having an Internet presence is critical for any successful campaign can brand you as "out of step" with one of the hottest issues of the day.

Because effective use of the Internet is all about connecting people with virtually unlimited information and opportunities for both on- and offline action, the task of breaking out potential uses of it into stand-alone categories is almost impossible. The same e-mail list you put together to use for notifying supporters of your upcoming speech in River City can also be used when you want to solicit funds. The Web site where you post press releases and the transcripts of your speeches can and should include information on how people can volunteer—and give them the opportunity to sign up right then and there to do so. It should also provide them with a vehicle they can use to make online donations. It makes more sense to us to consider the Internet's potential in this area in terms of two loose groupings—information/communications, under which we'll address campaign organization and volunteers, and fundraising. We will also touch very briefly on the topic of online voting. In the last section of the book we'll address yet another way the Internet factors into public life in America: its impact on the business of government.

To give you an overview of the Internet's potential as a synthesizing tool in your campaign arsenal, let's start with a few thoughts from Rich Galen, the former executive director of the Republican-oriented, and sometimes controversial, GOPAC. Galen understands that, in this new world of the Internet, "Anyone is everywhere, all of the time."

☆

The most common lament of candidates for public office is this: "I can't get my message out." This complaint had some currency over the last three decades when electronic advertising became the single most important method of contacting voters. Typically candidates who were either (a) the incumbent, (b) independently wealthy, or (c) well known from other endeavors prior to becoming a candidate had a tremendous advantage because they could raise the necessary funds or could write a check out of their own account to buy enough television and/or radio advertising to "get their message out."

The candidate who was the challenger, or had to begin his or her campaign from a dead start, has been at a disadvantage—perhaps an insurmountable disadvantage.

Now comes the Internet and the ability to "get one's message out" at almost no cost. To do a standard "campaign update" mailing to one thousand potential supporters will cost a campaign $330 in postage and, depending upon the printing and paper costs, perhaps another $100. In a campaign for president that is an asterisk. In a campaign for state representative in a rural district, that could be up to 50 percent of the total budget.

A good e-mail list, built by attendance at Rotary, Lions, and similar club appearances; by having supporters supply ten e-mail addresses each; by having a simple but attractive Web page, allows this candidate to do weekly updates at no marginal additional cost to the campaign.

Thus, a campaign can "get its message out" in a more efficient, more targeted, more personal way than even the most heavily funded opponent.

RESEARCH

The Internet, because of its vast reach, can provide a level of research to campaigns previously unimaginable in all but the largest statewide or national campaigns.

A candidate who needs information on, say, road infrastructure spending, can find federal, state, and, in many cases, county-level data with a few clicks of the mouse.

Preparing for a debate against an incumbent allows a challenger to check on the opponent's voting record, search for public statements, look at bills sponsored or cosponsored (especially at the congressional level) and puts the challenger on a level footing with the incumbent.

The campaign can also check local, regional, and major statewide newspapers every morning because so many papers have Web sites on which they put almost all of their printed material. In this way the campaign can respond to breaking news stories without waiting for the often-spotty reports from supporters in sections of the district or state far from the campaign headquarters.

The clever campaign in the 2000 cycle will hire a smart high school or college student to be the campaign Internet researcher under the guidance of the manager or communications director.

The Internet will prove to be the "great equalizer" that campaign finance reform, which would alter the way in which money can be raised and spent, will never do.

If even the least well-financed candidate can "speak" to as many voters as the best-financed candidate—which good use of the Internet provides—we will have made great strides in improving the democratic process.

THE INTERNET AND INFORMATION

There are three firsts and foremosts when it comes to using the Internet as a way to disseminate information about your campaign: a) have a Web site that is already up and *functioning properly* the day you formally announce your candidacy; b) make sure it's interactive; c) know how to utilize the power of electronic mail (e-mail).

Why have a Web site? Well, as we said before, not having one, or having a poorly constructed or constantly malfunctioning one, is one sure way to label yourself as out of touch with the way many of your constituents live their lives. This will become even more true as the "digital divide" continues to close. But to approach it more positively, having a Web site ensures that you have at least one medium of public communication available that affords you total control over what is said about you. Get used to thinking of the Web site as a central repository for all of the information you want communicated publicly about the campaign. Everything you would tell somebody about yourself in person, tell it to them on the site. Every speech you make, mention the site address and then put the transcript on the site. Each press release you issue to the media, put it on the site, as well—and the site address on the release. As we've said earlier, the press is growing more and more to rely on the Internet as a way to gather information; not only will your supporters (and potential supporters) be able to use the Web site as a way to quickly find out your stance on property taxes, so will the reporter who is trying to verify the information your opponent is putting out about *your* position on that issue!

Interactivity is critical for a couple of reasons. Again, it's what people are used to—they want to be able to click in one spot and send you a message about their thoughts on a given issue. It's also the way they can tell you they are interested in getting involved with the campaign; once you have a supporter's e-mail address, you can then regularly and personally update him or her on ways to provide on- and offline support to the campaign, be it through donating funds or coordinating a door-to-door campaign in a certain neighborhood. (Interactivity of course also comes into play with fund-raising; we'll address that in a moment.)

Lynn Reed, who owns NetPoliticsGroup.com, managed the 1996 Clinton-Gore reelection Web site and was the Internet consultant to former U.S. senator Bill Bradley's Democratic presidential campaign in 2000. She says the power of using the Internet to communicate to and with supporters first became widely recognized in the 1998 Minnesota gubernatorial race, when former pro wrestler and then-Reform Party candidate Jesse Ventura came seemingly from out of nowhere to take his state's highest office. "The lesson that most of us who do this for a living learned then was about the use of e-mail for organizing," Reed says. "They collected names and used the people on the e-mail list very effectively to do the jobs paid staffers would've done on a larger, better-financed campaign." By February 2000, the Bradley campaign had signed up more than one hundred thousand volunteers online. "That's a significant number of volunteers, and we communicated with them regularly by e-mail," she notes. "Every day, depending on where they lived, we asked them to do up to fifteen to twenty timely, meaningful things we needed them to do 'on the ground.'"

The campaign of Republican candidate McCain did the same thing, says its general counsel Trevor Potter, a Brookings Institution fellow and former chairman of the Federal Election Commission. "The Internet gives the campaign significant opportunities to reach its own supporters, tens of thousands of people at almost zero cost," he says. "Before it was a very people-intensive process, and quite costly by comparison." After McCain's surprise win in the New Hampshire primary, his campaign used the Internet to sign up more than fifty thousand new supporters in one week. "There's no way before the Internet that a campaign could have even acknowledged in one week fifty thousand people who were interested," Potter remarks.

Research, advertising and polling are other areas in which the information/communications aspect of the Internet can prove of vital assistance.

A candidate who needs information on, say, road infrastructure spending, can find federal, state and, in many cases, county level data with a few clicks of the mouse. The challenger who goes online to prepare for a debate against an incumbent can check out the opponent's voting record, search for public statements, and look at bills sponsored or cosponsored (especially at the congressional level) by the opponent; essentially, the Internet puts the challenger on a level footing with the incumbent.

A campaign can also check local, regional and major statewide newspapers every morning because so many papers have Web sites on which they put almost all of their printed material. In this way the campaign can respond to breaking news stories without waiting for the often-spotty reports from supporters in sections of the district or state far from the campaign headquarters.

In the 2000 campaign, both candidates McCain and Bush, along with numerous incumbent senators and congressmen, used the services of Aristotle Co. to engage in online advertising. While the company, which describes itself as "essentially a consultant on this new technology," won't provide specifics on exactly how it services its clients, it basically uses permission marketing to target Internet users who are registered voters. For a fraction of the cost of direct mailing or television advertising, the candidates can have their ads "pop up," seemingly at random, on Web sites unrelated to the campaign and hopefully grab the attention of the unsuspecting surfer. We expect to see a tremendous number of companies get into the online advertising business in the coming years, but don't think this method of advertising will by any means totally replace direct mail and/or television advertising. All the methods complement one another (especially when you put your Web site address in every commercial and on every piece of printed material and/or paraphernalia associated with the campaign!).

The interactive aspect of a site can come into play in another way with advertising. Most candidate sites now feature campaign merchandise people can order online: buttons, yard signs, hats, etc. The

McCain 2000 campaign site also featured such free downloadable items as bumper stickers. Again, we expect to see a great deal more of this in the very near future, especially in down-ballot state and local races where every penny must count twice!

Internet polling is another industry that, while it has yet to come into its own, is developing rapidly. Already there are companies that can organize focus groups and issue polls via the Internet almost instantaneously to help candidates make decisions on tailoring their messages; imagine the impact this is going to have on the way we make decisions about public policy.

The Internet and Fund-Raising

As we said, Internet interactivity also comes importantly into play with fund-raising. It's hard not to get excited about the fund-raising potential of this tool when Bradley's campaign by late February 2000 had raised $1.8 million via the Internet, and McCain's Internet total at the time was at a self-reported (and somewhat amazing) $6 million—especially when you consider that neither total included the Federal Election Commission-approved match. But as we've said before, no smart candidate should go into any race—be it for the local school board or for president—relying upon the Internet as his or her only mechanism for raising funds. Yes, each campaign should have a method by which supporters can contribute online, and we will out-line some critical reasons for that. But the candidate still has to do the hard offline work of asking in person, and the last time we looked, the importance of effective television advertising hadn't diminished in the least, either. And, bottom line, if people aren't excited about your campaign and the message you're sending, it doesn't matter if you plaster your Web site address on every bumper sticker and billboard in Kansas and provide people with eighteen interactive donation methods. They have to have a *reason* to want to give, and you have to provide them with it *before* you encourage them to donate online.

Phil Noble & Associates, an international political and public affairs consulting firm, added an Internet and new technology division in 1994. It has since evolved into PoliticsOnline.com, which among other services offers a usage fee-based mechanism for online fund-raising. Phil Noble says the interactive Internet capabilities his company is set up to provide to political candidates makes his group "the arms merchant for the Internet political revolution."

☆

Look at what happened with John McCain after New Hampshire. When New Hampshire happened he got a boost; he got $4 million and 40,000 people who said, "Hi, I want to help," instantly, automatically—in one place at one time. They could give money, volunteer, be given assignments.

In 1984 I was working with Gary Hart and the exact same thing (a surprise win of the New Hampshire primary) happened. But we couldn't get the damn envelopes open fast enough to get the money out and into the bank in time to buy media in the next state. Moments! Moments! That's all it takes now instead of weeks. McCain's Web site enabled him, once he got the momentum, to be competitive with Bush, to get enough money and enough people. "Hot today, in business tomorrow," that's the way it works now.

Why should any candidate devote time and resources to online fund-raising?

You get the money quicker.

If someone writes you a check, it takes days for the check to clear (that is, if it clears at all!). With an online donation, which is always made by credit card, by the close of business you literally have instant money in your account.

You spend less time and money raising the money.

Webmaster Max Fose, who worked on McCain's campaign, has been quoted repeatedly as saying it's 66 percent cheaper to raise money online: $100 spent for every $1,000 raised, instead of the traditional $300 to raise $1,000 through direct mail. And even if you do use your offline efforts to drive people to donate online, it's still more efficient to receive credit card donations than checks; people don't have to open those envelopes Noble was talking about, and, again, you have near-immediate access to the funds.

You frequently get new money, and sometimes even more money.

The problem with direct mail solicitations is that they're usually being mailed to a list of previous donors, whether to your campaign or someone else's. These people aren't new to the political process, and may in fact be so jaded that they throw out your carefully designed mailer without even opening it. The advantage of someone using your interactive Web site is that he or she has *chosen* to be there, and recent surveys of people who've used this method to contribute to a campaign reflect that many of them are in fact first-time givers—and that those who aren't are giving more online than they would have in response to a direct mail solicitation.

THE INTERNET AND VOTING

Mark our words, the reality of online voting is just around the corner. The technology already basically exists; it's just a matter of dealing with the issues of security and voter fraud. The first step will be online voter registration, and after that it's Katie bar the door. It's exciting to ponder the ramifications this will have on the political process as a whole. We believe online voting will not only greatly increase voter turnout, it will also move this great country further along the continuum from republic to sheer democracy. For example, right now the openly stated reason so many states resist public initiatives is cost. (The privately stated reason is that legislative bodies don't want to give up any more control than they have to, but that's a topic for another time.) When states can quickly and cheaply hold online referendums, and when citizens can vote on issues and for candidates 'round the clock from the comfort and privacy of their own homes, we believe the people truly will get government they deserve—one that is representative of their desires.

SECTION

"INSIDER TRADING"

THE ADVANCED SECRETS ABOUT CAMPAIGNS
THAT EVEN THE EXPERTS DON'T LIKE TO DISCUSS

We said from the start that this business of political campaigns is a secret world unto itself. And, just like in the world of finance, with its "insider trading" and those quiet (but illegal) "insider tips," there is an entire world of advanced, intricate, and often undiscussed "insider" moves that take place in political races of all sizes. And here is our big disclaimer: We don't endorse a great deal of what we're about to disclose; we just know it happens, and an alert campaign staff should be prepared.

THE TRICKS OF
THE TRADE

1. It's All About Turnout, Suppression, and Money

Here's where the true dirt and slime of politics hit the road—or should we say the street. Because winning any election has less to do with how many people like the candidate and everything to do with how many people turn out to vote for the candidate. Here are some of the most common methods used to control voter participation.

Street money

It's one of the oldest tricks in the book. Few people really believe it goes on, but we're here to tell you it does. Money is collected, either from legitimate campaign or PAC funds, and dispersed to legitimate organizations such as churches, unions, or charitable or civic-minded organizations. The money is usually distributed by someone who controls a certain geographic or political group. A large portion might go to the leader of such an organization as a gift or consulting fee. Often, the larger distributions of funds intended for "street" operations are reported on disclosure forms. But once these larger blocks of funds are in the hands of those who will distribute them, there is less accountability and often no evidence of where the money has gone.

Here is where the money usually ends up:

★ As "gifts" to ministers, civic leaders, or other individuals influential in the community in exchange for their active endorsement and for getting their followers to the polls to vote "the right way" on election day.

★ As money to "drivers"—individuals who drive cars or vans all day, searching out people in their area who will vote a preprinted "ballot" in support of a given candidate.

★ As small cash tips given to individual voters to go to the polls and vote the "ticket" that is listed on the preprinted ballot.

Are we proud to know this goes on? No. Is it illegal? In some instances it probably breaks or at the very least skirts the law. But there are clever experts who are able to make the transfer and distribution of street money legal in many instances.

It should be noted that street money tends to be used in larger races. But it can have an impact on the smallest of contests, particularly in general elections, by turning out a larger partisan vote than would otherwise show up at the polls.

And what are the amounts of cash involved in these races? Try millions of dollars. In some large states, the street money "distributors" have been at it for so long that they have a virtual monopoly on the business. In others, the money is distributed more strategically, based on who is powerful at a given time in a given race.

Voter suppression

Just as money is used to turn out certain segments of the electorate, it can also be used to keep certain voting blocs away from the polls on election day.

How does this work? In its most blatant form, street money tactics are employed to get church and civic leaders to discourage their voters from turning out. The message can be oblique, such as "I'm so sick of both these candidates that I don't care who you vote for," or the more obvious "We need to send so-and-so (or the so-and-so party) a message by not going out in that rain on Tuesday and being taken for granted."

In its more sophisticated form, suppression is proliferated through targeted media attacks (radio, mailers, etc.) that employ well-respected names to trash a certain candidate in a given community.

2. The Secret World of Poisoning the Well, or At Least Confusing the Voter

Campaigns must protect themselves against last-minute offensives designed to fly "under the radar," efforts that allow the opposition to viciously attack without being caught playing dirty.

The negative advocacy poll and the "slick sheet"

One of the sneakiest ways of poisoning the well against an opponent is the use of what is normally called "advocacy polling." It goes something like this: The phone rings in a household about four days before the election. A registered voter, who may well have already been identified through earlier calls as supporting or leaning towards candidate Smith, hears the following:

> Q. "In the race between Mr. Smith and Mr. Jones, if the election were held today, for whom would you vote?"
> A. "Mr. Smith."

Q. "Would it change your vote to know that Mr. Smith has twice been accused of beating his wife, has been treated for drug abuse, and that he filed for bankruptcy two years ago?"

Get the picture? The respondent thinks he or she is answering questions in a legitimate poll. This is a crafty way of delivering extremely damaging information—true or untrue—directly to the voter.

Many candidates send out "slick-sheet" mailings just days before an election, hitting their opponents with damaging negative material—again, true or untrue—and hoping that there isn't enough time for them to reply.

In the 1980s and '90s, certain conservative religious-oriented groups would distribute hundreds of thousands of "scorecards" or endorsements in churches—and on cars parked near churches—the Sunday before an election. Although many ministers have refused to allow political material to be distributed on church grounds, this practice continues in some areas.

Voter confusion

Voter confusion is also a very dangerous trick. It is well known that Republicans often have a hard time convincing African Americans to vote for them. One top GOP consultant told us of a little-known tactic in which thousands of leaflets are distributed on election day (or just prior to) with the name of a white GOP candidate in bold letters, accompanied by the picture of an attractive African American. Underneath the picture (or on the back), the leaflet says in small type "Pictured is Walter Thomas, Co-Chairman of the Smith Campaign." The hope is that some percentage of voters will be confused and vote for a white Republican whom they believe to be African American.

Another tactic used to generate voter confusion comes in the form of "the battle of the sample ballots." For years, political parties, unions, and other organizations have printed and distributed "sample ballots" designed to lead the masses to vote for their candidates. In the Kinko's world we live in, such ballots can easily be copied in color and texture with the selected names replaced to support the opposing ticket. If distributed in the same areas and to the same voters as the original samples, these "ballots" cause confusion and reduce the effectiveness of the original sample ticket.

3. The Sucker's World of Political Debates

Nothing gets more attention—or has less of an impact on an election—than a political debate. Preparation for debates is tedious and time consuming, and the public rarely focuses on them except in presidential races, where the first debate usually has some impact (and the subsequent debates do if someone really falls apart in the first one—like Reagan did against Mondale in 1984).

Generally speaking, though, debates are best used as a means of distracting your opponent if you enjoy a major lead in fund-raising and political advertising. The hope is that the opponent will spend all of his or her time preparing for an event that, even if televised, will have few viewers—while the leader continues to rake in money and buy more paid advertising, the kind that wins races.

There is a flip side to this as well. Candidates in the lead (often incumbents) can sometimes make the mistake of agreeing to too many debates, thereby giving an otherwise unknown candidate too much legitimacy and additional name identification. There is the story of a congressman in the early 1980s who was seeking reelection and decided to challenge his unknown opponent to "a debate in every city in the district and on all three television stations in the area." The unknown candidate suddenly began to rocket up in the polls because of the free name recognition he was receiving from the debates. The incumbent had to raise more money so he could defeat what would have otherwise been an unknown opponent.

If a candidate must debate, our advice is basically the same as what we recommend when giving speeches and press conferences in general:

★ Use the "three issue approach" in opening and closing statements.

★ When you get a question you can't answer, go back to the most relevant of your three main issues.

★ Be sure to memorize a few facts and statistics.

★ Always number your answers.

And finally, our secret debating tip guaranteed to get a rise out of the competition:

★ Whenever your opponent gets heated or attacks you, be sure to laugh a little and remind him or her to "calm down and stick to the issues." This will infuriate your opponent and make you appear cool and collected.

If you must debate, be sure to hold a practice debate with a moderator or questioners that follows the format of your actual debate. No matter how badly you might perform in the practice round, it will make your actual performance much better.

4. Elections Really Can Be Stolen

"We were robbed" is an oft-heard remark after a sporting event. Unfortunately, it can also be applied to the world of politics, where voter fraud has become an increasingly serious problem.

PIERRE: A few years ago, while I was still lieutenant governor of Georgia, a colleague called needing my help. It appeared he had been defeated by just a handful of votes. I immediately dispatched an election attorney to the district, where a proper inquiry showed that boxes of ballots had gone uncounted, with many absentee votes still sitting at the post office. The election defeat was reversed into a victory.

There are far too many cases these days of improper procedures at America's polling places: voters being given incorrect instructions by workers; failures by workers to check voter IDs (required in many states); and even nonvoters or noncitizens voting because of a lack of worker vigilance.

To prevent such wrongdoing, candidates should be prepared to send poll watchers to police election sites regularly. Select trusted people for this watchdog role. In minority polling places, it is often wise to have your own minority poll watchers in order to challenge any problem from the opposition. The local board of elections should be alerted to any problem (as well as the police, if necessary). Poll watchers in fraud-prone precincts should be armed with camcorders so they can record any incidents. They should also carry cell phones so they can immediately call a local or state board of elections official. Sometimes, for example, candidates knowingly or unknowingly violate the designated area around a polling place for campaigning and displaying paraphernalia. If this space is violated and the board of elections officials at the site look the other way, then a senior elections board member, the police, and even the media should be alerted.

The campaign manager should line up volunteer poll watchers months beforehand for most, if not all, precincts. Usually the local or state elections office conducts periodic training sessions to instruct new poll workers and inspectors, and your candidate's volunteers should be encouraged to attend.

If a candidate or campaign manager is suspicious of certain precincts, there is a simple, inexpensive way to check the address of a suspected fraudulent voter. About two weeks before the election, mail a first-class letter to the voter at the suspect address. The face of the envelope should say "Please do not forward" and a return address must be printed on the envelope. The mailing need not be identified as coming from a political campaign. Retain any letters returned "undeliverable" as proof in case the suspected fraudulent voter later appears at the polls. It is also smart for a campaign to keep a volunteer lawyer on hand in case there's a need to immediately initiate legal action (impounding a precinct's ballot boxes, for example).

The tedious task of counting paper ballots, even with a computer, can last a few hours, depending on how far-flung the precincts are from the central election office. It is essential that a candidate have poll watchers checking these procedures. Once, in the 1980s, a female ballot counter with long fingernails was spotted punching holes in certain paper ballots from a heavily Republican precinct— thus spoiling those ballots and keeping GOP numbers down. Poll watchers should be suspicious if there is an unusually large number of spoiled ballots.

In another race in 1996, a candidate actually got away with sending people to cast ballots for dead voters! (The scandal was uncovered later, and the perpetrators were convicted.) Poll watchers might want to periodically check with the elections office to see if it has faithfully purged the names of registered voters who have died or have moved away and are unqualified to vote.

Absentee ballots in particular should be policed. These ballots are for people who have legitimate reasons for being out of town or are incapacitated. There have been cases of unscrupulous campaign workers going into nursing homes or hospitals and coercing patients into voting. So an abnormal number of absentee ballots from a precinct should be carefully scrutinized. (Look especially for what could be forged signatures.)

Many precincts are won or lost by just a few votes. Therefore, if a candidate's poll watchers have prevented even a few bogus voters from casting ballots, it could mean the difference between victory and defeat.

5. Preclusion, Turnarounds, and Harassment

These odd-sounding terms are all real problems in the world of politics in the new millennium.

Preclusion

This is an advanced tactic ignored by far too many candidates, especially those who enjoy a large lead in fund-raising. Perhaps the greatest example of this preemptive move was the Democratic National Committee's combined effort with the Clinton reelection campaign of 1996. After the Republican Congress forced a shutdown of all but essential government services in a budget standoff with Clinton, Democrats seized on the issue. Realizing that the GOP's likely presidential nominee would be Senate Majority Leader Bob Dole, the Democrats began running ads months before he received the nomination, pointing out the failures of the Republican Party and hanging the name of the increasingly unpopular Gingrich around the neck of the relatively popular Dole.

The Republicans sat by silently, month after month, while the Democrats precluded Dole from ever getting his campaign off the ground. By the time Dole won his party's nomination, Clinton enjoyed an insurmountable lead; the public had been preemptively brainwashed. The lesson here is that if campaigns can afford to bury their opponents early, they should definitely do so.

On the bright side, anticipated negative attacks against your campaign can often be minimized by utilizing preemptive tactics.

Self-disclosure on your own terms—prior to disclosure by an opponent—can often help soften the blow. But there's one big caveat about self-disclosure or preemption of negative information: If the negative attack against your campaign or candidate cannot be proved, you have no duty to disclose it. Candidates with an otherwise sterling record of public service have disclosed piccadillos that probably would never have come to light in the legitimate press—and have lost as a result. Sometimes preemption can backfire.

Turnarounds

Remember that opponent who kept saying "government should be run like a business" and "people are having to pay too much in taxes"? Well, it's a perfect opportunity for a "turnaround" when you discover that same candidate failed to pay his business license or his sales taxes. A turnaround is taking your opponent's issue or moral high ground and using it against him in an attack on his or her past business or other civic transactions. A good campaign will constantly search for "turnarounds" that can keep the opponent on the defensive and undercut his or her credibility, without getting into the private life of the candidate or their family.

Harassment

It used to be that harassment of the opposition was unthinkable. And pure verbal abuse or obvious attacks turn the voters off. But in recent years there has been a drift towards a more subtle method of mental gaming: following the opponent around with a camcorder. The purpose is allegedly to capture the speeches and statements of the opponent, but the true intent is to harass. Such tactics must, of course, carefully avoid trespassing and other related statutes. But since candidates must campaign in public places, such harassment can never be escaped for long. The strong candidate counters this move by going up to the camera at every stop, making a little joke, or smiling to demonstrate that it isn't bothering him or her. But the smarter move—if affordable—is to have someone counter-record the individual who is doing the harassing. Indeed, they might even want to pursue the harassing video cameraman to his or her favorite public locales. After all, as long as it's legal, turnabout is fair play.

6. The Secret Fund-Raising Machine

Here's an insider's trade secret that very few candidates really learn. If they find the courage and discipline to do it, it can be the single greatest logistical move a campaign can make. It involves the dreaded phoning for funds—but it takes it to a new level.

In order for this system to work, the candidate must have access to an office separate from campaign headquarters. The room should be equipped with a large desk for the candidate with multiline phones, a second desk adjacent to the candidate's, and a third desk in an opposite corner of the room.

Two assistants sit at the desk adjacent to the candidate, holding profile cards of potential donors, including names of spouses and personal information. (The cards have been prepared in advance.) The person at the desk on the other side of the room has a master list of individuals to be called—hundreds, all in sequential order. He or she begins by placing the first call: "I have Tom Jones calling for Ms. Peak." If Ms. Peak takes the call, an assistant hands Ms. Peak's profile card to the candidate. After two minutes of conversation, they signal it's time to ring the next caller. Once a new potential donor is on the line, a hand signal is given to one of the assistants sitting adjacent to the candidate. They signal him or her to "wrap it up" and ask for the donation. Then the next card is shoved in front of the candidate seconds before the new call is transferred.

This system can operate like clockwork, each individual called believing that he or she is known intimately by the candidate. And the additional key is to have "runners," volunteers or a small paid staff, willing to go immediately to the individual's house or office to pick up their pledged check. Wrap up each conversation with "Can we get that check today? I'll send so-and-so out to pick it up."

WHEN THE REAL
WORLD OF BUSINESS
MEETS THE MEAN
BUSINESS OF POLITICS

Here's a basic truth that would seem hard to believe: Most lobbyists and governmental affairs experts have a strong incentive to see their clients' issues linger on unresolved for years. Why? Because they make more money if an issue drags on for years instead of months. And, to make matters worse, they try desperately to make their clients believe what they do is so mysterious that no one could possibly challenge the effectiveness of their endless strategies and meetings. This is particularly true in Washington, D.C., where projects often attract teams of fifty, sometimes one hundred, lobbyists, many of whom are more interested in getting their contract renewed than in getting the job done.

The unfortunate truth is that these professionals are usually necessary. While most corporate CEOs and officers believe they understand politics, few really do. But there are a few secrets, at least, that non-lobbyists can learn that will allow them to make better decisions with regard to their companies' governmental affairs efforts:

★ Never give money to a politician without requiring a one-on-one meeting, even if getting that meeting requires giving more than you otherwise might.

★ Never contribute to a fund-raising event beyond a nominal amount, unless you (or your corporation) are part of the sponsoring group. You will get lost in a sea of contributions designed to make someone else look good.

★ It is better to host a fund-raising event than to donate to one. This is particularly true if you believe in the candidate—or his or her chances of winning—and can host the event on your home turf, or can make sure you or your representative is master of ceremonies. Candidates remember those who host and speak. And, even more importantly, be sure to be the one who gathers the campaign checks and (assuming it doesn't violate any local or state campaign laws) hands them to the candidate personally.

★ In major races, such as for governor, U.S. Senate, and certainly for president, never believe that a thousand-dollar check will be enough to make you or your company stand out. It puts you in the candidate's corner, but not on his or her mind.

★ It's better to give to promising candidates who will lead in the future than to jump on the bandwagon of a well-established politician who will view you as a newcomer and "just another supporter."

★ Never believe that simply because your company is a major corporation or important local business you will have influence with a candidate, particularly an incumbent. There are some national companies who could have lots of clout but don't contribute to political campaigns. And they wonder why nobody is bending over backwards to do them any favors!

★ Never give money or anything else to an elected official who demands it in exchange for taking (or not taking) action in your favor on a given matter. This goes on in the world of politics more than anyone would like to admit. But giving in to these demands is not only illegal; it's stupid. Once a dirty politician (we believe the number of dirty ones is actually pretty low) realizes that he or she can hold you "hostage," they will never stop. Dishonest types seize on weakness, and usually respect honesty and strength—so be sure to remain strong.

We are often amazed by the lack of strategic planning that corporations and other entities demonstrate with regard to governmental relations, what should be a critical aspect of their business. Many companies and organizations seem to believe that they can compensate for their own lack of political contacts or public awareness by simply hiring a representative or lobbyist who will give them instant access and credibility.

While many companies take this approach (and many lobbyists take their money), the reality is clients gain little from this arrangement. Unless the organization has a detailed strategic plan—just as they would for marketing a product or implementing a new piece of equipment—their "governmental affairs" efforts are usually not worth the money and time spent.

So how does a company or organization make sure it gets taken seriously in this delicate interplay between the private sector and politicians? Here are a few pointers that even the most savvy, Gucci-loafered lobbyist might overlook (or at least not share).

★ Find a small number of elected officials and create a true bond with them. The biggest mistake that people interested in persuading elected officials make is in believing that they need to give money to a wide range of politicians. Giving campaign donations or personal attention to everyone only means that there will be fewer resources to go around. It's far better to have a small cadre of bright, honest, good friends in elected office than it is to have a multitude of acquaintances who don't really know your company, your cause, or you.

★ Leverage the power of your political friends. So many "governmental affairs" experts fail to recognize that influence is not limited to those who write checks, give fund-raisers, or are political activists. Indeed, the greatest power is found between those who play the game "inside the locker room." Elected officials need one another. There are more true debts on the floor of a legislative body or city council than you would ever find in the world of corporate contributions. The smart company learns how to find elected officials who are their friends and who truly believe in their issues. Hopefully those officials will use their political capital to persuade colleagues to share their view on issues important to that company or other entity.

★ Use all of your resources. It is amazing how many companies and groups have unique resources but are unwilling to share them with political figures. For example, the most highly prized possession in big-time politics is a safe and reliable airplane. Because of federal and state restrictions, even the most important political leaders need to have a wide array of airplanes for campaign and fund-raising trips. Yet many corporations view the use of a corporate jet or other plane as productive only if it is carrying essential executives from their own company. How shortsighted. Allowing a politician to use a plane for a fund-raiser is an investment of friendship that can have a major effect.

★ Most politicians in the new political world build their base by raising money and giving support to other political candidates. Newt Gingrich and Bill Clinton rose to national prominence by giving both ideas and money to fellow elected officials within their respected parties. Now, virtually every member of Congress who aspires to a position of leadership within their caucus or conference raises or gives significant money to colleagues in tough reelection contests. But it's still the true pros who can really pull it off—and they are the ones who almost always move up the political food chain.

THE INTERNET AND LOBBYING

We hope that by now you so clearly understand our position that politics should be conducted in a businesslike fashion that you never want us to mention it again. We think it's very important to note that we also believe that businesses should adopt more of a campaign mentality in the way they deal with government. This includes adopting some of the leading-edge systems, which we talked about earlier, that politicians are already embracing: advocacy via the Web, monitoring of issues via the Web, and fast-paced communication via the Web. Companies should be utilizing twenty-first century Internet-based technology not only for the business of conducting business, but to influence the legislative and regulatory bodies that make crucial decisions that affect the commercial world.

In our offline political consulting business, we've found, sadly, that people are often shortsighted in terms of how they factor in the influence government really has on the way business gets done. The laws passed by Congress and the state legislatures comprise only a small portion of how government—the one business that will never go out of business—impacts the financial aspect of people's lives.

Many otherwise-savvy business executives fail to consider what up until now only the most inside of insiders have known about, and traded on: the mechanics of how city contracts—to handle gas, water, cable, you name it—get let; the way that environmental regulations get constructed behind the scenes before they are ever even discussed in a public setting; the timing on the issuing of millions of dollars in state bonds. We could go on, but we think you get the picture.

As we said at the beginning, we have taken our traditional consulting partnership online in an effort to bring the equalizing power of the Internet to play in the arena of political affairs, working with individuals and businesses to transform how the business of government gets done. No longer are small companies automatically cut out of the game because they can't afford the fees of a name lobbyist; a service such as this enables the mom-'n'-pop shops to find out the same intelligence on issues of concern to them as what the big dogs on their block are hearing from their "people on the Hill." It also allows the big dogs to independently confirm what they're hearing from their lobbyists.

The Internet is all about providing something of value faster, and at a lesser price. In the world of lobbying, information *is* that something of value, and delivery doesn't get much faster than immediate, which is how quickly Web sites and e-mails can communicate on any given matter.

Dan Solomon is publisher of NationalJournal.com, the online home of National Journal's publications, including *National Journal* magazine, the *Hotline* and *Congress Daily*. Because the audience for his company's numerous online services includes policy makers and opinion leaders, NationalJournal.com holds a distinctive position in the political process:

It's the insider's insider. Here are some of Solomon's thoughts on how the Internet is changing the business of lobbying.

☆

As lobbying has generally changed from the practice of insiders talking to legislators to one in which more people are engaged in grassroots campaigning to persuade legislators, organizations are recognizing that they don't engage citizens only at the time of an election. The Internet has facilitated that process; organizations can reach out directly to people and explain what is important. They can reach more people more affordably.

Second, the Internet has opened up the government and allowed people to identify who they should lobby. Anyone can find out who to contact, from Congress down to the state legislature. They can put a name to a face and say, "Hey, that's my person," all through entering their zip code. It makes government more accessible.

And it makes contacting people much more easy. You can e-mail your member of Congress. From the Internet you can make a phone call or send a fax. The information and identification is all at one point, and so is the communication tool. No other medium can do that. With direct mail, it's here is the message, go somewhere else to communicate, and television advertising can't be as targeted and effective. And the Internet allows established organizations to form coalitions with constituencies, through e-mail and online advertising, without having to form formal coalitions with other organizations.

What will not change is that the Internet will not replace lobbyists. Smart lobbyists will use it to amplify what they do, and if they truly have influence, it will amplify that influence. Within the community there's been a great debate about the effectiveness of e-mail as a lobbying tool. That's not the point at all. The point is, is the Internet used in the process? And the answer is yes. Communication doesn't need to be Internet communication. You can engage in online organizing for offline communications.

Ultimately, it's just another tool in the bag, and it needs to be a tool that *communicators are comfortable with. Lobbyists aren't afraid to put up a television commercial even though they have no idea how a TV camera works. The Internet should be the same; it's about audience, about message, about what you want people to know and do.*

According to the Center for Responsive Politics (CRP), lobbyists spent $1.4 billion to influence federal officials in 1998. If that fact doesn't confirm for you that lobbying is big business, we don't think anything will. Now, thanks to the power of the Internet, this organization and others can use their Web sites to make data such as this available in a clear and understandable format, which contributes to a new—and we think healthy—sense of transparency to the business of lobbying. At www.opensecrets.org, for example, the CRP analyzes campaign contributions fueling every election cycle 2000 congressional and Senate race, including breakdowns by industry, geography, and top contributor. The Federal Election Commission's Web site, www.fec.org, includes data about political action committees (PACs). Some may perceive the Internet as a threat to the so-called smoke-filled backroom manner in which they've always conducted business with the government. We think that in the end this greater sense of openness about the process, and the inclusive nature of the medium, can only mean positive changes to a system that impacts almost every aspect of every citizen's life.

THE INTERNET AND GOVERNMENT

Perhaps nowhere does the Internet have the capacity to impact the life of the average citizen so much as in changing the way he or she does business with the government. The online possibilities, many of which are already realities, are endless: researching the status of a bill under consideration by Congress, reporting a pothole or malfunctioning streetlight to city hall, paying everything from speeding tickets to taxes, and, as we discussed earlier, voting and registering to vote.

In fact, Vice President Al Gore's National Partnership for Reinventing Government has as its stated goal to, by January 2001, "put in place the infrastructure to ensure that Americans will have access to all government information and be able to conduct all major transactions on-line by 2003." The White House is even online, at www.whitehouse.gov. Its site currently lists "Twenty Things You Can Do and Learn on U.S. Government Web Sites." You can find information on everything from how to start your own business to the quality of the water in your neighborhood; you can also access the Department of Housing and Urban Development's comprehensive "homebuyer's kit," and find help after a natural disaster from the Federal Emergency Management Agency.

There are already numerous private companies cropping up to offer Internet capabilities to states and municipalities; with names like EZGov.com and Gov.com, they are filling a market need to get governments online quickly, and we expect to see them flourish and prosper. As Solomon, the publisher of NationalJournal.com puts it, "Elected government officials will feel compelled to provide this. There will be political pressure from their constituents—'If Sears can do this, why not the city of Los Angeles?' Most people don't know what's involved in offering online services. But they see it all around them, and they'll expect it from government, as well."

We might add that our own company, InsiderAdvantage.com, has become a leader in providing proprietary information about government opportunities for businesses. It has become perhaps the most exciting venture into which we have ever entered.

GOVERNMENT IMPACT ON THE INTERNET

In the end, one of the greatest issues that business, government, and the American people will face is if and how to regulate this new and still-developing behemoth that will be one of our primary means of communication and commerce for the foreseeable future. To tax or not to tax? That's a particularly hot topic Congress addressed initially when it passed the Internet Tax Freedom Act in 1998, imposing a moratorium on any new Internet taxes until October 2001. It also created the Advisory Commission on Electronic Commerce and charged that group's members with coming up with recommendations on the matter during the year 2000.

What about First Amendment issues? Do slander and libel mean the same thing online as off? And presidential candidates in the 2000 election cycle have warned repeatedly of the perils of cyberterrorism and the wealthy/poor digital divide, also valid concerns.

We don't think we, or anyone else, can look into a crystal ball and tell you what the future holds for government regulation of the Internet. But we can predict this: The process won't be dull.

CONCLUSION

If all of those insider tricks make you feel cynical, join the club. We're both out of elected politics partly because we could only stand this mean business for so long. Elected officials are like a giant group of professional athletes, or members of a top-secret fraternity; we speak a special language in the "locker room" of politics that is the same no matter what your party or level of service. The names and faces all blur together after a while, and self-preservation is always the main concern. Threats make you mad; broken promises make you even more upset. You spend much of your day dealing with constituents, only to spend all night fending off phone calls.

But we figure you've heard enough partial commentary from us; it's time to turn to another seasoned political pro for some practical perspective and final advice for all would-be politicians.

Julian Bond has been a national figure since helping lead the civil rights sit-ins in the South in the early 1960s. He helped organize SNCC (Student Nonviolent Coordinating Committee) and was nominated for vice president at the 1968 Democratic national convention, withdrawing his name because he was too young to serve. He did serve for more than twenty years in the Georgia state legislature, both House and Senate—though initially the House refused to seat him because of his opposition to the Vietnam War. Elected in 1998 as chairman of the NAACP national board, he holds honorary degrees from nineteen schools and universities. He currently lives in Washington, D.C., where he is a Distinguished Scholar in Residence at American University. He is also a history professor at the University of Virginia.

☆

You can motivate voters to respond to your issues in a campaign in one of two ways. Either by convincing them that the other candidate is absolutely opposed to their interests and that, if successful, will take away whatever the interest is and weaken it. Or, by demonstrating that you, above all others, are committed to this interest. Now, these may sound like the same thing, but they mean to me either running a negative campaign in which you tear down the other guy, or running a positive campaign in which you may never even mention the other candidate and just constantly hammer away at how committed you are to whatever these interests are—that there is no one who cares about these things as much as you do. Now you can do both at the same time, but it really strikes me as a choice. I always try to do the second one, just to make myself the good guy, not even to mention the other candidate. But I think inevitably campaigns do both.

I actually don't think that campaigns are more negative today, as people sometimes say, because they have always been negative. Do you remember "Ma, Ma, Where's My Pa? Gone to the White House, Ha, Ha, Ha." That was directed at President Grover Cleveland in the 1880s. It is not that campaigns are more negative. I think they are more in our faces because of television and radio, so much media, so pervasive, so much more so than only a few years ago.

Anything you say, no matter how innocuous, can become a dagger in your heart in the skillful hands of some political consultant. So the candidate said this. Why didn't he say that? What did he mean when he said that? Or doesn't that sound like this? Yet it works the other way too. Look, if you will, at the George W. Bush campaign. How many photographs have you seen of him with black children? They're just everywhere. His campaign people put him in these situations when, if a picture is going to be taken, he's kissing some little black girl or he's got his arms around some black boy. He doesn't have to say a thing about civil rights or affirmative action or anything. All he's got to do is let the pictures speak. I think it's tremendously effective.

Bill Clinton's second campaign was probably the best I've ever seen, partially because he just seems to me to be the perfect politician. He is amazing. I've never seen anybody better with people, either when you see him one-on-one—it's only you, you are the only person in the world—or even when he's talking to a larger group of people. He seems to be talking right to you. It is genuine, I think. A gift, and he's got it. And he is also resilient. After the Monica story broke, all the television talking heads said it was all over, he was out, might resign at any moment. Now, I can imagine another person resigning, saying I can't put up with this, mentally and psychologically. But Clinton just bore ahead.

I don't know that Senator Bob Dole's campaign for president in 1996 was the worst ever but it was bad. It was surprising to me because he is a man who has been in public life for so long, and he just seemed not in it during the campaign. I don't know why. He has sometimes been a very effective partisan, extremely effective.

We have to find some way to get the big money out of campaigns. I don't know how you overcome the constitutional objections, but there has got to be some way.

Money is what is driving some of this meanness, some of the distortion. Now, if you took the money out you wouldn't have perfect politics by any means, because we are not perfect human beings. But it would make a tremendous difference.

The first thing I would say to anybody running for office is just simply, make sure your family is ready for this. Not because there may be hard times, but because a campaign engages everybody in the family. They are either out there on the campaign trail with the candidate or they are not going to see him or her for months and months and months. Then I would tell them, candidate and family, to make a real examination of themselves. Is there anything in their lives—and I'm not talking about scandal—but is there anything that you don't want talked about? Just as a matter of privacy. It doesn't have to be anything secret or something bad, but anything. Be sure it will probably be discussed during a campaign. Lastly, I would tell any aspiring candidate, make sure you are physically fit before you take that first step on the campaign trail.

As we believe our book has demonstrated, American politics is no longer a game to be entered into lightly. It is a hard-nosed battle zone that ranks right up there on the ugliness scale with the World Wrestling Federation when it comes to dirty tactics—and to selling an image that the people want.

Yet for every jaded ex-politician, there is a new crop of bright-eyed and idealistic young leaders ready to enter the fray and "change the world." We were those bright faces once, and we understand the lingering allure of the political arena. We also still believe that for our democracy to survive, we must have good people who are willing to make the commitment to public service. We have written this book not to discourage good people from politics but to arm them for the battle.

ACKNOWLEDGMENTS

WE'D LIKE TO THANK THE FOLLOWING PEOPLE:

Hal Gulliver, who conducted most of the interviews; Kristi Lamont Ellis, who assisted in the Internet sections; Scott Rials, who also conducted several interviews; Robin Williams and Williams Services, and Gary Reese, all of whom provided essential research materials and stories; Tysie Whitman, Burtch Hunter, and Scott Bard of Longstreet; Chuck Perry, Steve Gracie, and Debbie Roth; Tracy Modica, Matt's assistant.